When Ray Kroc invented McDonalds, his brilliantly creative mind asked: how do I eliminate the 80/20 rule in my business? His answer was, turnkey it, Stupid! And that's what he did. By doing so, he created a revolution, and while doing that, he turned the 80/20 rule upside down in his business.

Now you can do the very same thing. But, before you can do that, you have to, just have to, understand what 80/20 really is! You'll finally understand why most people's businesses don't work and what you absolutely, positively must do about it in yours.

You're in for one of those explosive moments when an interesting notion becomes a momentous epiphany because Perry Marshall is about to blow your mind! Read slowly. Put down often. Do what Perry says. Then we can all go out to lunch and celebrate!

—MICHAEL E. GERBER, AUTHOR, *THE E-MYTH*

If you don't know who Perry Marshall is—unforgivable. Perry's an honest man in a field rife with charlatans.

—DAN KENNEDY, AUTHOR, *THE ULTIMATE MARKETING PLAN*

Perry Marshall is a sales and marketing ninja. Read this book, apply the lessons, and slice your way to victory.

—CHRIS GUILLEBEAU, *NEW YORK TIMES* BESTSELLING AUTHOR, *THE $100 STARTUP*

Perry Marshall is the Gene Schwartz of the 21st century. Schwartz's book, *Breakthrough Advertising*, is every bit as current as the first day it rolled off the press in 1966. Perry's work is like that.

Perry has consulted with the best marketers on the planet for over a decade. He combines the attributes of the most calculated engineer with the artistry of a poet. He delivers the deepest dive into the "80/20 Principle" you've ever taken, as it applies to copywriting, buying traffic, scaling traffic, dominating markets, and sales conversion. 80/20 is not a rule of thumb; it's a law of nature and a way of life. If you are not following Perry's formula, you are leaving millions on the table.

—BRIAN KURTZ, EXECUTIVE VICE PRESIDENT, BOARDROOM INC.

Perry has been THE go-to wizard for using Google AdWords as the mega-valuable tool for entrepreneurs it was meant to be, and I recommend his materials without hesitation. Without his insights and advice on pay-per-click, I can't even imagine where many successful online business owners (in literally hundreds of industries) would be right now. Deservedly, Perry's now stepped into the mainstream and is no longer the best-kept secret of niche entrepreneurs. The unique tools in this book are game-changers for anyone looking to take their business to the next level.

—JOHN CARLTON, LEGENDARY COPYWRITER AND PRESIDENT, MARKETING REBEL INC.

Perry Marshall's teaching on 80/20 was so riveting I cancelled my appointments for the afternoon and read the entire manuscript. It is a gold mine in insight and depth. I am still processing it!

—LANCE WALLNAU, PRESIDENT, LANCE LEARNING GROUP

I've read well over 1,000 business books and *80/20 Sales and Marketing* is among the top ten for actionable strategies to fast impact your bottom line. Every business person should own a copy—highlighted, dog-eared, and underlined.

—BILL HARRISON, CEO, BRADLEY COMMUNICATIONS CORP.

Best business book I've read this year. Focusing only on the 20 percent of the 20 percent that really matters, using the power curve, and reverse thinking has made my business extremely profitable. Once you understand how to disqualify, work less, and make more, life flows naturally. Powerful, little-known concepts are clearly articulated with terrific real world examples and concise summaries.

—James Schramko, Founder, SuperFast Business

Very often, the most powerful ideas in the world are laying around in plain sight unappreciated, poorly understood, and unused.

One such idea was Google's AdWords system. It may be hard to believe now, but for many long months after it was released, this ingenious new approach to advertising—which now amounts to about about 90 percent of Google's prodigious income—was dismissed by the pay-per-click advertising experts of the time.

The Pareto Principle is another idea that contains incredible, but largely untapped power. Many have heard of it, usually as the 80/20 Rule, but until recent years it was one of those 'so what?' factoids that most people fail to appreciate let alone do anything with.

Amazingly, the same guy who first sorted out how to use Google AdWord's profitably, is the very same guy who has breathed fresh life into this most productive of mathematical insights.

If you are a marketer or business owner, or anyone who wants to be more successful in this world, wrapping your head about the 80/20 Rule as it is explained by Perry Marshall will be the single most effective thing you can do all year, any year.

—Ken McCarthy, CEO, Amacord, and Founder,
The System Seminar for Internet Marketing

Every once in a while, a book arrives that seems to speak the right message at the perfect time. *80/20 Sales and Marketing* is one of those books, and one that will prove to be a milestone in the marketing canon.

I hadn't finished the first few pages before I knew beyond doubt that I was reading something that would be extremely significant for my business, and my life. I barely blinked before I was halfway through!

Perry Marshall has delivered a work of simple genius. He reveals a pattern that is so woven into natural law that, when you open your eyes to it, you'll see it all around you.

Leaving no stone unturned, he then takes you by the hand through a complete business master class, covering marketing, personal effectiveness, time management, advertising, cash flow, hiring, firing, loving the work you do, and making a real difference.

I can safely guarantee that 20 percent of this book will take your success to the next level, and within that just a few gems will skyrocket you to another place completely.

—BEN HUNT, AUTHOR, *CONVERT!: DESIGNING WEB SITES TO INCREASE TRAFFIC AND CONVERSION*

Perry's 80/20 course was of those pesky life-changing experiences. Now I'm heading off to go do it.

—RANDALL INGERMANSON, AUTHOR, *WRITING FICTION FOR DUMMIES*

You will be stunned how scary accurate the Marketing DNA Test is.

—BRAD RICHDALE, LEGENDARY WRITER, DIRECTOR, PRODUCER, AND DIRECT MARKETER

We have started using the DNA test on all candidates we interview, and it seems to be remarkably accurate and insightful. I say this with some qualification, having taken assessments by DIVINE and a DISC profile not too long ago. MarketingDNA stands with the big boys!

—HANS RIEMER, PRESIDENT, MARKET VANTAGE, LLC

When I was a kid, my favorite board game was Chutes and Ladders. I loved it when I landed at the foot of a ladder and could take a short cut to victory. Reading *80/20 Sales and Marketing* gives me the same feeling. Though Perry and the rest of us look at the same world, he sees the hidden order of things—the ladders to success that almost nobody recognizes.

He's taken the 80/20 Principle farther than it's ever been taken before, and shares tools so powerful that I challenge anyone to implement these insights and not quintuple their business within two years.

—HOWARD JACOBSON, AUTHOR, *GOOGLE ADWORDS FOR DUMMIES*

There are a lot of smart marketing gurus out there. At one time or another, I've been on most of their email lists and spent five figures on their products. But, if I had to choose just one to listen to, it'd be Perry.

If you only pay attention to Perry Marshall when it comes to AdWords, you are missing the boat. From copywriting to conversions to email auto responders and much more, Perry has proven himself to be one of the most astute direct marketers and business strategists, online or offline, around today.

—ADAM KREITMAN, WORDS THAT CLICK, CRAZYEGG.COM

The fact that I have my own TV show in Poland is directly connected with Perry Marshall's 80/20 Productivity Express.

—GREGORY MOGILEVSKY, TV HOST, *BIZNES W SIECI* (*BUSINESS IN THE NET*) ON TVN CNBC IN POLAND, WARSZAWA, POLAND

I took Perry's 80/20 course last year and had the most productive year of my life. No exaggeration.

—MICHAEL ARNOLD, PRESIDENT, THE NATURAL FERTILITY EXPERTS LTD, LONDON, UK

As of today for 2013, my client base is down 23 percent; revenue is up 43 percent. It's like I was in second gear for a year, and now I'm in fourth. More speed, less RPM.

—Adam Libman, Libman Tax Strategy

I bought the Perry Marshall marketing system quite a few years back, his book, *Ultimate Guide to Google AdWords,* white papers course, and a few other very useful courses and seminars and implemented them.

I went from working all the time and killing myself to all of a sudden making more money, starting a second and third business and having a huge amount of time off when I wanted to! I still do a lot of work, but on my terms now.

—Jade Sullivan, Access Trading

I'm a productivity junkie, and I've done just about every book, training, or system, from Stephen Covey to David Allen. Perry's course has been some of the best teaching on this subject I've ever experienced. In the first session, I reclaimed an extra hour per day; by the third session, I totally revolutionized how I run my business.

I was too busy to take it. Ha ha—I took it anyway. Cut my average workweek by about 20 hours and more than doubled, almost tripled, my income.

Brought on two major, six-figure clients. Have two more knocking at my door right now. Literally booked solid. Fully on track to clear $1 million in revenue for this year.

Made room for me to become a major contributor in my church, but not the way you think. Yes, we give money, but what I'm speaking about is the fact that I've been free to lead financial peace classes and be available in other ways, for my church.

Stopped doing things that I was good at, but that were not the highest use of my time—a major leverage point.

—Ray Edwards, Founder and CEO,
Ray Edwards International, Inc.

80/20

SALES AND MARKETING

The Definitive Guide to Working Less and Making More

PERRY MARSHALL

Foreword by Richard Koch, author of the bestsellers
The 80/20 Principle and *The 80/20 Individual*

Ep

Entrepreneur
PRESS®

Entrepreneur Press, Publisher
Cover Design: Andrew Welyczko
Production and Composition: Eliot House Productions

This publication is designed to provide accurate and authoritative information
in regard to the subject matter covered. It is sold with the understanding that the
publisher is not engaged in rendering legal, accounting or other professional services.
If legal advice or other expert assistance is required, the services of a competent
professional person should be sought.

Library of Congress Cataloging-in-Publication Data
    Marshall, Perry S.
      80/20 sales and marketing : the definitive guide to working less and making
more / by Perry Marshall.
      p. cm.
      ISBN-13: 978-1-59918-505-7 (alk. paper)
      ISBN-10: 1-59918-505-9 (alk. paper)
      1. Marketing—Management. 2. Sales management. I. Title.
      HF5415.13.M3635 2013
      658.8—dc23   2013011847

Printed in the United States of America

17 16 15 14   10 9 8 7 6 5

To the Master Mathematician, and to Vivian.
"Wisdom was created before all things, and the understanding
of prudence is before all time."
—Sirach 1:4

Contents

Foreword
by Richard Koch

Author of the million-copy selling classic *The 80/20 Principle* and *The 80/20 Manager*

I'm really pleased to write this introduction to *80/20 Sales and Marketing* for three reasons.

With the exception of my own books and the astonishingly brilliant book by Tim Ferriss, *The 4-Hour Workweek*, this is the first addition to the canon of books about the 80/20 Principle (hereafter "the Principle").

Now, why should that matter? Because as Tim has said, the Principle is "the cornerstone of results-based living." When you realize that it is *small* causes that have *big* results, life becomes an exciting voyage of discovery. Suddenly, every day brings a liberating quest—to find the small things you can do, in very little time, with very little money or none at all, to have a big impact on the people around you.

This applies to everyone and to everyday life—a smile, a hug, a sincere thank-you, a word of advice that is just right for someone who is struggling or suffering, a practical task that takes you only 10 minutes but would take someone else an hour or forever to do—these are examples of interventions that everyone can manage.

Equally important, the Principle makes us aware that there are small things we all do that have a hugely negative impact for our friends, family, and work colleagues. Just to stop doing these small things can change lives.

Though some uses of the Principle are obvious and take almost no mental effort, other applications of the Principle take quite a lot of thought to realize in the first place. And this is where people who have devoted years of their life to thinking about the Principle can help.

Such people—starting of course with Vilfredo Pareto, the Italian economist whose research into wealth creation sparked the original discovery, but also extending to quality guru Joseph Juran and a host of people in the computer industry, notably Steve Jobs—can make a dent in the universe by thinking about applications of the Principle and then making these available to anyone who will listen to them.

Once the original thinking is done, the application of the Principle is easy.

Perry Marshall stands in that tradition. He has something original and extremely useful to say, because he has thought profoundly about the Principle and how to apply it to an area—sales and marketing—that nobody else has cornered.

Do not be deceived by the easy, bouncy style that Perry deploys. This is a person who has spent time delving deeply into the mysteries of 80/20 and come up with some original insights that are literally priceless. There is a lot of wonderful wisdom in the book you now hold.

My second reason for joy at this book is that Perry takes a hint that I originally made about the Principle—its "fractal" nature—and expands it, drawing some incredibly powerful conclusions. What does this mean?

Well, think about leaves or coastlines. A leaf has the same pattern on it whether you examine it with the naked eye from a distance, or close up, or take a magnifying glass to it. You see the lines and veins, and they look the same whatever the perspective. Similarly with a coastline—all coastlines in the world are different, but they are all recognizably the same pattern, and this applies whether you see the coast up close or from a jet plane.

And with the 80/20 principle, the thing is that it applies all the way along the length of any distribution. So, for example, if 20 percent of roads in your area carry 80 percent of the traffic, it will still be true that if you disregard the 80 percent that carry little traffic, the 20 percent that carry most will still be subject to the Principle. Twenty percent of the top 20 percent of roads will carry 80 percent of the traffic *among the top 20 percent of roads.*

Let me say that again slowly. If 20 percent of roads carry 80 percent of traffic, roughly 20 percent of the 20 percent—that is 4 percent—of the roads will carry 80 percent of the 80 percent of traffic on those roads. In other words, 4 percent of the roads will carry 64 percent of the traffic. And so on.

To be honest, I hadn't quite grasped the implication of that until Perry's book hammered it home to me. That is, we benefit most from the Principle when we apply it at its upper reaches. If 20 percent of our time gives us 80 percent of our useful output, it's still true that a fifth of that 20 percent will contribute 80 percent of the results within that "useful" category—in other words, there are some things that take *almost zero time* that are incredibly valuable.

If we want to make the world better, we had better work out what those unbelievably leveraged activities are. Nearly always they are decisions we make and stick to.

To take another example, one of the most valuable things any businessperson can know and use is that, almost certainly, a fifth of our customers are responsible for four-fifths of your profits—or something similar. Sometimes 20 percent of core customers actually account for fully 100 percent of profits, and the rest on average are—if you analyze their true value—loss makers. *You would be better off without them.* Once you realize this, business becomes a heck of a lot simpler and easier.

But the fractal point Perry makes is that 20 percent of the 20 percent of customers are ultra-valuable, at least potentially. Four percent of the customers may account, or could account, for 64 percent of profits. If you know who these customers are and provide them with what they really want, all you have to do is double sales to them and you have another 64 percent of revenues.

And Perry's point, as you'll see, is that very often these sales are not consummated, *simply because you don't have the very expensive products that these ultra-valuable customers really want to buy.* Sales and marketing, therefore, begins with product development—for your very best and most enthusiastic customers. This is a huge insight.

Of course, you can't charge several times as much for the same product—though Starbucks, some would say, tries hard. You have to provide equivalent value, so if a product is 10 times as expensive, it must give at least 10 times the value.

But very often, it costs you less than 10 times as much to provide that value. And it is certainly easier to grow by selling more to your existing happy customers than it is to find new customers who will love what you do.

Let me make this real by giving an example from my life—long past, thank God—as a management consultant. Around 1980, I left one great consulting firm—the Boston Consulting Group (BCG)—to join a small offshoot called Bain & Company. Bill Bain, the founder, believed strongly in the Principle. He kept telling us, "Your best new customers are your existing customers."

Instead of pursuing new business wherever it could be found—a natural temptation for the new firm on the block—he told his people to look within their client relationships. He discovered a new and much more intensive way of consulting with a few firms at incredible depth.

Whereas the two leading consulting firms in the world at that time—BCG and McKinsey—would think a relationship that garnered $1 million dollars a year was a good one and wouldn't try to multiply that number, Bill Bain and his partners did.

For them, if a client was being billed $1 million, there was in most cases no reason why they couldn't be billed $10 million or even much more—provided Bain & Company delivered the value to justify that. And that we could easily do by working with the chief executive to transform the company, using the incredibly powerful insights that strategy consultants, thanks largely to BCG, had developed.

Bill Bain reasoned that if $1 million of consulting could deliver $5 million of value, then $10 million could deliver $50 million of value, or maybe much more. For a big client, there was no artificial barrier. Though he never expressed it this way, value delivered to a client was fractal. By focusing on a few terrifically powerful causes of profit improvement, the sky was the limit, both for the client and for the consulting firm.

Now, as Perry will show you, the sky is the limit for you and your firm, if you truly understand and use the Principle, in ways he will explain.

The third reason I love this book is that it is open-ended and experimental. It will get you to open your mind and think about doing things you have never done, and about ways of doing what you are already doing in totally novel dimensions.

So that is enough from me. Get on with reading the book now. Perry's enthusiasm is infectious, and I hope you go down with a big dose of it! One thing I am sure of—if you read this book with an open mind and use your brain a bit in thinking about its most powerful points, you really can change your business and your life.

—Richard Koch
Cape Town, February 2013

Richard's new book, The 80/20 Manager, *has just been published. It describes 10 ways that managers can transform their work lives and results without extraordinary effort.*

Introduction

My trusted friend Ken McCarthy recommended Richard Koch's landmark book *The 80/20 Principle.* A few days later, it arrived in the mail. I took the book to my favorite hangout, Buzz Café.

I got to page 14, and my mind suddenly lit on fire. Yeah, I'd heard about 80/20 before. I knew the "Pareto Principle": How the Italian economist Vilfredo Pareto noticed that 20 percent of the people owned 80 percent of the wealth. I knew that 80 percent of your sales come from 20 percent of your customers. Up to that point I'd thought it was mildly interesting.

But suddenly I saw an entirely new and different dimension: 80/20 APPLIES TO EVERYTHING! A thousand new connections formed, connections I'd never made until that very instant.

Recognizing that I had just stumbled upon something that was absolutely huge, I broke into a cold sweat.

I jumped in my car and raced home. Fifteen minutes later I was sprawled out on the living room floor with a calculator and papers scattered all over. The dots were connecting faster than I could write them down.

My wife, Laura, came home and said, "What happened to YOU!?!?"

Koch's book, which I had just begun to read, would prove to be the most pivotal business book I'd ever picked up.

But there was something else, too: I'd experienced an epiphany, a *new* insight about 80/20. One that I've never read about in any other book before or since. Suddenly I saw 80/20 *everywhere*. It was like flipping a switch and witnessing the world change from black and white to color.

This book is about the contents of that epiphany. It's how it became possible for my business to expand a thousand percent and more. It's about the myriad ways I began to apply 80/20 in every aspect of sales and marketing. This new insight became *the* organizing force of my professional life.

It was a huge key to me cracking the code on Google's advertising system a full five years before most other people did; 80/20 was also instrumental in me becoming the world's best-selling author on the hyper-competitive subject of AdWords.

80/20 helped immensely after people had optimized every possible part of the ad campaigns and needed to know what to do next; it helped later when it was time to decode Facebook advertising. I've written about 80/20 in every business book and taught it in nearly every training course. I can't imagine doing a business consultation without it. It led to the creation of a tool, included with this book, that radically altered my entire concept of sales and marketing.

If you're just starting out in sales or marketing and you dig numbers, this book is your new bible for what actually works in sales, marketing, lead generation, publicity, and ecommerce—and what doesn't. 80/20 will become your number one way to organize everything else you ever learn about selling for the rest of your life. You'll get to the *dinero* two times, even five times faster. You'll pocket more of it, too.

If you're a seasoned sales or marketing pro yet you know you haven't reached your full potential, this book offers an elegant new framework for every move you make. It will amplify every skill you've acquired so far.

You'll be able to immediately and reliably estimate how much money you're leaving on all your different "tables." You'll find levers within levers, the ability to produce not merely 2X but 100X improvements in productivity. You'll gain x-ray vision into untapped markets and you'll "see around the corner" in ways that surprise your colleagues and competitors. You'll effortlessly move into regions of higher effectiveness.

Finally, you can apply 80/20 to your reading of this book! You can read 20 percent of this book and get 80 percent of the benefit, because this book is marked with special sections called "Pareto Points" and a logo that looks like this:

Watch for this icon as you read, because it means the material is *extremely* important.

Also, you'll want to visit www.perrymarshall.com/8020supplement and print out my "Double Pareto Page"—the top one percent most powerful strategies in this book, condensed into a punchy one-page hot sheet.

I believe you'll find these shortcuts to be so valuable that you'll want to read 100 percent of the book and the online bonuses, then reread all of it—because if the best one percent impacts your income by $100,000 or more, the entire book is easily worth $250,000. This book will change your life.

Yes, I know that's a bold statement. But test me and see if it's true, because I've tucked many dozens of strategies and powerful techniques into the coming pages.

I've been teaching 80/20 to my "Planet Perry" members for 10 years now—people who subscribe to my emails, join my mastermind groups, and attend events. Thousands of sales professionals and entrepreneurs have internalized these techniques and built successful, thriving companies, sales and consulting careers around it. Today, I offer it to you.

—Perry Marshall

How 80/20 Works and Why

A few years ago I held a seminar in Chicago called "The 80/20 Seminar for Direct Marketing." To my knowledge it was the first such conference or seminar. It cost $3,000 to attend and I had about 80 people in the room. All of them ran businesses of one kind or another, most of them online. To illustrate the all-pervasive nature of 80/20, I said, "Everybody stand up if you have shoes on."

Everyone stood. I said, "If you own fewer than 4 pairs of shoes, please sit down." A bunch of people sat down, and about 50 were still standing.

"If you own fewer than 8 pairs of shoes, sit down."

More people sat down, about 30 left.

"If you own fewer than 16 pairs of shoes, sit down."

Thirteen people, 9 of them women, still standing.

"32 pairs of shoes."

Three women standing.

I smiled. "Don't be embarrassed, ladies. Just tell the truth, cuz I'm illustrating a principle here. How many of you have more than 64 pairs of shoes?"

Two sit down. One left standing. She cringes with embarrassment.

"How many shoes do you have?"

"Umm, about 80."

"Thank you so much. You can sit down now. Give this woman a hand!"

Everyone clapped. "20 percent of the people own 80 percent of the shoes. Can you see that?" I said. All nodded in agreement.

"Everybody stand up again—everyone who owns at least one domain name." They were all marketers, so it was pretty much everybody.

"Sit down if you own fewer than 10."

Half the room sits down.

"Fifty."

Half again sits down. We've got maybe 20 still standing.

"Two hundred."

A bunch more sit down, 10 standing.

"Five hundred."

Five people left. I keep going—1,000, 2,000, 5,000.

At 5,000 domain names, I've got two people left. At 10,000, one guy sits down.

Mickie Kennedy from Baltimore, one of my best customers, is the only one left standing. "How many domain names do you own?"

"Twelve thousand."

Mickie was a "Domainer," the domain-name equivalent of flipping real estate. He owned entire portfolios of domain names, some selling for tens of thousands of dollars.

20 percent of the people owned 80 percent of the domain names, **and in a room of 80 people, one guy owned nearly half.**

Almost everything is like that.

Not absolutely everything—but most things. Shoes, domain names, Bible verses, trips to Vegas, pearl necklaces, consumption of dinner napkins, tubes of lipstick. Rabbit populations, streams and rivers, size of cities in southern Argentina, passengers on London's underground "Tube" trains. Net incomes, profit margins, software development timelines. Foreclosures, trips to the tavern, and trips to the emergency room. Diameters of stars and planets, and the size of craters on the moon.

Why rattle off this scattered list of things in a business book? Because if you can see 80/20 at work in this list, you can identify it in any part of your business. Once you've learned to recognize it, you can't *not* see it. Look at the tree outside your window: 80 percent of the sap travels through 20 percent of the branches.

If you have 30 customers, you're tempted to treat them all the same. Well they're really not the same at all. Odds are, 20 percent of your business comes from just one of them. The size of those customers really looks like this, in Figure 1–1.

All these things obey the 80/20 principle. That's because 80/20 isn't a mere rule of thumb, and it's not just for business. It's a law of nature. John Paul Mendocha observed that 80/20 is literally *the* "Invisible Hand" that Adam Smith wrote about in his landmark book, *Wealth of Nations*, when Smith made his case for free-market capitalism in 1776.

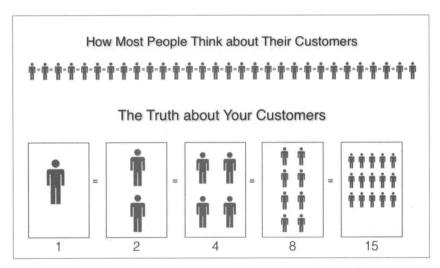

Figure 1–1. Customers are notoriously unequal. If you have 30 customers, their capacity to spend money with you looks like this. The first customer generates 20 percent of your business, the next two largest give you the next 20 percent, and so on. The same principle of inequality applies to almost everything in your business. (Illustration by Danielle Flanagan.)

It's not the exact number 80/20 that's the rule; it's the principle of *positive feedback,* which is when behavior is rewarded so that it produces more of the same behavior. Sometimes it's 60/40 or 70/30; sometimes it's 90/10 or 95/5. The exact numbers aren't so important. But it's always there.

It's a law that almost nobody ever gets taught in school. In fact, our current educational system trains most of us to be blind to it, ignore it when we do see it, and even fight it as our enemy, instead of embrace it as our friend.

Exceedingly rare is the person who truly understands it in all its depth, and I discovered a new insight, a new approach that I've never found about 80/20 anywhere else.

Almost nobody reads simple election statistics that "14 percent of the voters turned out at the polls in this election" or "5 million people donated at least $5 to the election campaign" and translates it into a vivid, meaningful picture of those people, all the way from casual interest to rabidly passionate and addicted.

Few people ever even consider that a tiny minority of the donors give almost all the money. And that the one million smallest donors gave less money than the top ten.

Even if you've got average math skills, in literally 60 seconds you'll be able to predict, with spooky accuracy, that 735 donors gave that same election campaign more than 10 grand—with a simple web page you can pull up on your smartphone.

If your job has anything to do with raising money, you better darn well know that those 400 donors exist, what they look like, and where to find them.

It might also be useful to know that there were 17 donors who gave over $250,000.

With some very simple tools that come as a bonus with this book, you can punch in a few numbers on your phone or computer in seconds, and make spooky-accurate guesses. How many gave over $5,000? You'll know.

At lunch on the back of a napkin, you'll be able to shuffle through all kinds of ordinary facts about your business—how many customers, how many VIP members, how many shoplifting incidents, the number of people who opened yesterday's email. You'll easily assign dollar figures to all and instantly know which opportunities are worth pursuing and which ones waste your time and money.

80/20 101

80/20 says 80 percent of your results come from 20 percent of your efforts, and 20 percent of your results come from the other 80 percent.

But that's barely the tip of the iceberg. The *real* power in 80/20 is that you can disregard 80 percent of the roads in your city, only look at the top 20 percent, and the 80/20 rule will *still* apply. 80 percent of the 80 percent of traffic is on 20 percent of the 20 percent of roads.

That means 64 percent of the travelers drive on 4 percent of the roads. That's $80/20^2$.

Then we do it again: 80 percent of the 80 percent of the 80 percent of the traffic, runs on 20 percent of the 20 percent of the 20 percent of the roads.

In other words 52 percent of the travelers drive on 0.8 percent of the roads. That's $80/20^3$.

And it just keeps going because 40 percent of the drivers are driving on 0.2 percent of the roads: $80/20^4$. 32 percent take 0.016 percent of the roads. That's $80/20^5$.

80/20 says that if you have 10 rooms in your house, you spend almost all your time in two or three of them. It says if you hire 10 salespeople, two will generate 80 percent of the sales and the other eight will generate only 20 percent of the sales.

That means that *person for person,* the two are SIXTEEN TIMES as effective as the eight. That's right—a good salesperson isn't 50 percent better, he or she is 16X better. That means there's huge leverage in 80/20: much to be gained if you pay attention, much to lose if you don't.

The Leverage Power of 80/20 Is in the Layers

$80/20^1 = 16:1$
$80/20^2 = 250:1$
$80/20^3 = 4,000:1$
$80/20^4 = 65,000:1$

$80/20^5$ = One million to 1

. . . and so on.

If you're *not* a math person, stick with me and I'll make this abundantly clear. This is relatively simple and HUGELY important, because if you want to *influence* that traffic—say, sell them something by putting up a billboard—you can accomplish as much with one billboard on a major expressway as 100,000 yard signs on residential streets. That's just a simple, elementary example of leverage. As the story unfolds, you'll discover far more.

You can climb as high as you want, until you run out of roads or customers or products or people. If you have enough numbers to run 80/20 five times, your winners are a million times better than your losers. That's million-to-one leverage, and it's not a joke. It's reality.

Here's a perfect example. Consider the wealth of the entire world—20 percent of the population enjoys 80 percent of the wealth:

According to the International Monetary Fund, the total gross domestic product of all 196 countries in the world in 2011 was $79 trillion (refer to Figure 1–2).

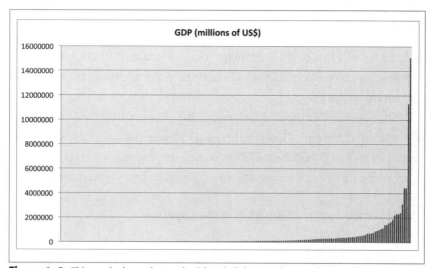

Figure 1–2. This graph shows the productivity of all the world's countries from least to greatest. Sixty-three percent, or almost $50 trillion of that $79 trillion, comes from just 10 countries. So 63 percent of ALL wealth is generated by 5 percent of the countries.

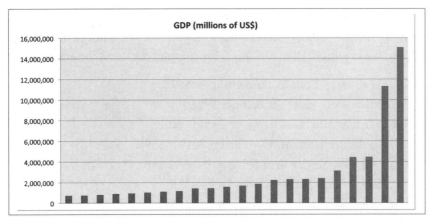

Figure 1–3. 80 percent of the world's wealth is concentrated in 22 countries.

There are 196 countries in the world, and over 63 trillion (80 percent) of those dollars come from just 22 countries. So, as shown in Figure 1–3 (page 7), 80 percent of the world's wealth is concentrated in just 9 percent (196 countries divided by 22) of the countries.

I want you to notice how the shape of the curve is the same, whether we're looking at the whole picture (Figure 1–3), or just the top 20 percent (Figure 1–4), or just the top 4 percent. As we move forward, that curve is going to become very useful to you.

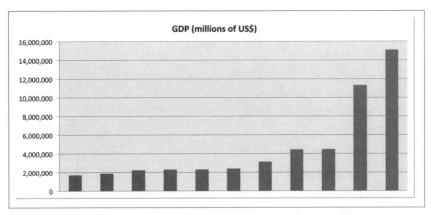

Figure 1–4. Zooming in, we see that $15 trillion, or 19 percent of the total $79 trillion, comes from one country, the United States. So 19 percent of world wealth is generated by 0.5 percent of the countries. (REF World Economic Outlook Database, October 2012, International Monetary Fund. Accessed on October 10, 2012. Graphics by Lorena Ybarra.)

Now consider the top 10 wealthiest people in the world. I took this from the Forbes 400 list, from *Forbes* magazine 2011. I lumped members of families together (all the Waltons are lumped together, for example):

1. Walmart—Four Walton children $87B
2. Microsoft—Gates & Ballmer $72.9B
3. Koch Brothers—Charles & David $50B
4. Berkshire Hathaway—Warren Buffett $39B
5. Google—Sergey Brin & Larry Page $33.4B
6. Soros Fund Mgt—George Soros $22B
7. Las Vegas Sands—Sheldon Adelson $21.5B
8. Bloomberg—Michael Bloomberg $19.5B
9. Amazon—Jeff Bezos $19.1B
10. Facebook—Mark Zuckerberg $17.5B

The total is 381.9 billion, and the top three own 55 percent of it.

80/20 is true of the world's seven billion people—and it's still pretty much true of the top 10 wealthiest people. The 80/20 pattern is exactly the same whether we're looking at the world's seven billion people, the Forbes 400, or the 10 richest people in the world.

Best of all, 80/20 and $80/20^2$ are true of almost *anything* you can measure in a business:

- Sources of incoming phone calls
- Effectiveness of salespeople
- Sales to customers
- Physical location of customers
- Popularity of products
- Types of product defects
- Problem employees
- Customer service problems
- Sources of conflict
- Shoplifters
- Activity patterns in a 24-hour day, or a week or month
- Performance of distributors, affiliates, and channel partners
- Sources of web traffic
- Advertising waste

- Advertising effectiveness
- Productivity of web pages
- Reasons customers buy

That means every one of these things is a source of leverage. It means that each has multiple layers of leverage that you can obtain by "zooming in"—$80/20^2$ (250:1) and $80/20^3$ (4000:1). It means you can combine many of these factors together and cut huge amounts of waste out of your day and your budgets.

As we dive into this material, I'll give you a software tool that makes eerily accurate predictions and "sees around the corner" in ways that will mystify your friends and colleagues.

Everybody's Counting the Wrong Stuff

Did you ever take a test in high school and listen to the teacher explain the results of the test? "The average was 77, the low was 41, and the high was 99." Sometimes my teachers would draw a bell curve on the board, like the one in Figure 1–5.

But if you're a results-oriented person, the bell curve almost never tells you what you really *want* to know or *need* to know. Let me explain.

One hundred students took a science test. The average was 77. The 77 is important to the teacher and the school, but it's not all that important to

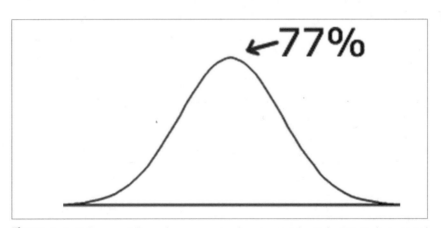

Figure 1–5. Bell curves tell you how many people got a certain grade. "12 students scored between 80 and 89 on the test."

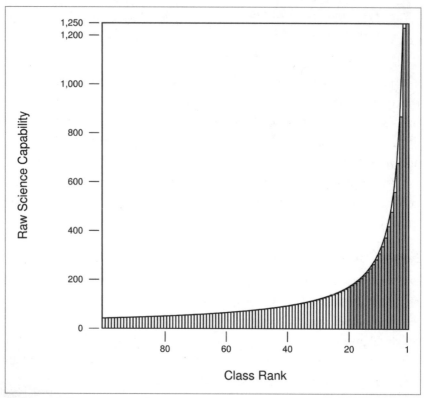

Figure 1–6. The 80/20 Power Curve.

anybody else! If you took it and got an 87, great, you know you were above average. But let's say you want to hire one kid to do science experiments. You want to know a) which kid is the best at science, and b) how good is he, really?

If you're trying to get something done, if you care about *achieving results,* there's a much better way to see this class and everyone who took the test. Let's put the kids on the **80/20 Power Curve** (which you can access www.8020curve.com), in Figure 1–6.

You have lived in and around the 80/20 Power Curve every day of your life. But it hasn't been until now that you actually saw what it looked like. Almost everything that matters to you in your life follows this curve.

The Power Curve shows the data very differently than the bell curve. It ranks everyone from bottom to top, like the bell curve does. But it's different from the bell curve because it doesn't measure how many of them got a certain score. It measures how good they are.

So the x-axis is students ranked from bottom to top. The y-axis measures their ability; their ability to do science, or write, or read, or play basketball, or whatever.

It shows you that 80 percent of the science capability is carried by 20 percent of the kids. In fact, if you look a little closer, you will see that the best kid has 50 times the "science horsepower" as the worst kid, and 14 times as much as the average kid. In this graph, the average is 77, but the top is over 500. This is because the very best kids could answer far more difficult test questions for extra credit and get a score of 500 percent or 1,000 percent.

Recruiting Power Players

The Power Curve also shows you one other thing that the bell curve doesn't even hint at: the tremendous capacity of the very best. Let's say the top student in the class got 100 percent and the next one below him got 98 percent. Is the best student really 2 percent better than the second best student?

In the school of hard knocks, where passion and performance are far more important than answering questions correctly, the best student is probably *50 percent better* at science than the second best. Not 2 percent better. This is incredibly important. If you care about curiosity, discoveries, research, commitment, and results, recruiting the best instead of second best is huge.

For you, the talent scout, the test was an easy way to sort the winners from the losers. I'll give you a powerful illustration of that in a few pages.

Average Is . . . Average

80/20 is unconcerned with "average." Why? Because almost nobody is average, and the ones who are don't matter much anyway. Instead of emphasizing mediocrity, the Power Curve focuses on ability. It zeroes in on the best, the cream of the crop.

By the way, "A" players are usually picky and demanding. They tend to be prima donnas and break a lot of rules. They need special care and feeding. Your number-one sales diva, who outsells everyone else three to one, may insist on having her own private dressing room, a masseuse, and a personal feng shui consultant. That's just how "A" players are. If you don't like that, you can always hire "B" players and be mediocre, if you prefer.

In business we talk about "averages" all the time. Average transaction size, average number of customers who walk through the door every day, average number of purchases, etc.

And while those are convenient handles that everyone knows how to grab on to, those numbers almost never tell you what's really important. Like which are the top 20 percent of transaction sizes? Who are the most important customers walking through the front door? Who makes a lot of purchases, instead of just a few?

The 80/20 Power Curve is far more useful than the bell curve. You need to resolve to stop thinking in terms of averages. Instead, think in terms of extremes and multiples, exponential growth and powers of ten.

The Power of Power Laws

The math that drives 80/20 is called power laws. A Power Law more or less says that if foxes are 10 times bigger than rabbits, you can expect 10 times more rabbits than foxes. And if horses are 10 times bigger than foxes, you can expect 10 times more foxes than horses. On it goes, down to the smallest of insects and even bacteria.

Power Laws tell us that an accurate picture of cause and effect is best expressed in powers of ten. They tell you that your customers' ability to spend money is not in increments but multiples.

The Richter scale measures earthquakes. It's based on Power Laws. A 5.0 on the Richter scale is barely noticeable. A 6.0 is 10 times more powerful, likely to knock objects off of shelves and might cause injuries. 7.0 is 10 times more powerful than that, enough to level homes and buildings and inflict loss of life.

The 1-to-10 Richter scale is a far more useful way of expressing the power of earthquakes than regular numbers, which would have to be one to 10 billion. Imagine a radio announcer saying, "Last night's earthquake had a strength of 100,000. Fortunately, almost nobody noticed."

There are no world-famous 5.0 or 6.0 earthquakes because they're not even big enough to shake you awake in the middle of the night. But the 2010 earthquake in Haiti was 7.0. The devastating San Francisco earthquake of 1906 was 8.0.

5.0 earthquakes are 10 times more common than 6.0s, which are 10 times more common than 7.0s.

Decibels measure sound the way the Richter scale measures earthquakes, except every 10 decibels signals a 10-times change in power. A range of 0 to 120 decibels is a lot more manageable and intuitive than a billion-to-one range in power. Decibels convey how your ears perceive sound much better.

To see cause and effect in your business as it really is, shift your business thinking. Business is not about increments. It's about the Richter scale and powers of 10.

PARETO SUMMARY

▷ The real power of 80/20 is $80/20^2$, $80/20^3$, and so on. It keeps going until you run out of things to count.

▷ 80/20 applies to everything in the world that has positive feedback, from the income of 7 billion people to the Forbes 400.

▷ Almost everyone talks about "average," but average equals mediocrity. The 80/20 Power Curve is about results.

▷ Top performers are not twice as good as average performers. They're more like 100 times better.

▷ Everything that really matters in business isn't linear, it's exponential. 80/20 is about Power Laws—powers of 10. You should always think in multiples of 10.

Rack the Shotgun

Pareto
Point

At age 17, my friend and colleague John Paul Mendocha dropped out of high school, hitchhiked to Vegas, and hustled for four years as a professional gambler. Every day, 50,000 people were showing up in Sin City expecting to go home with some loot. John resolved to do his very best to ensure that the city lived up to its reputation as "Lost Wages."

A teenager running loose on the Las Vegas strip quickly figures out he needs some street smarts, so he found himself a mentor. Rob was a seasoned gambler who took John under his wing in exchange for a split of the proceeds.

"Son, the first lesson about gambling is, you have to play games you can win. You need to play people who are not as good at poker as you are. Those people are called *marks*.

"Get in the car John, I'm gonna show you something."

Rob took John to a cabaret. They walked in the door and sat down. Hard rock was pounding at 110 decibels, women were snaking around dance poles, and everyone in the club was greedily absorbed in alcohol and entertainment.

Rob had a sawed-off shotgun in his jacket. He carried it everywhere he went.

He pulled the shotgun out, slipped it under the table. He pressed the lever, popping the chamber open as if to load it. But instead of inserting a shell, he loudly snapped it back shut, with that sharp, signature ratcheting sound shotguns are famous for—what enthusiasts call "racking the shotgun."

A few heads in the crowd twisted around, trying to see where the *racking* sound had come from. Everyone else was oblivious, absorbed in their haze of nightclub revelry. Then Rob slipped the gun back into his jacket.

Bill, the owner of the club, slipped over to their table. He asked Rob, with a tone of concern:

"Everything OK over here, boys?"

"Everything's fine, Bill. Just teaching the lad a lesson," Rob replied. Then he leaned over and said to John, "John, the people who turned around—*those* guys are *NOT* marks. Do *not* play poker with them.

"John, your job is to play cards with *everybody else*."

That, my friend, is how you harness 80/20: I call it *racking the shotgun.*

You send one calculated signal that most ignore, but a few to respond to. You might not even have to make that move yourself. Someone else can rack the shotgun—you just have to *watch*. It separates the 80 percent from the 20 percent. 50 people in the club; 10 heard the shotgun sound, forty didn't. Fastest way to separate the amateurs from the pros.

Before you bet your precious time or money on any sales, marketing, or business endeavor, you need to rack the shotgun.

Rob racked the shotgun to *disqualify* the street-smart few—the ones who KNEW what that sound meant—and to qualify the many. But if he'd been looking for candidates for a skeet-shooting retreat in Montana, the guys whose heads whipped around would be qualified. They'd be the ones most interested in your retreat.

Everything you do with your customers racks the shotgun.

If you've racked the shotgun by offering, say, a troubleshooting guide, and 50 people have turned their heads by requesting it, you can rack a different kind of shotgun—like offering a live training workshop. This narrows your 50 down to 10 hyper-responsive targets who will carry you farther than the other 40 combined.

Please understand, 80/20 is not about "marks" per se, or whatever shady stuff that goes on in Vegas. There's an 80/20 in *every* situation. 80/20 is about the fact that everywhere, all the time, in every company, school, church, household, and supermarket aisle, every Facebook page and email list, people are self-identifying as being the *right* targets or the *wrong* targets for you. 24 hours a day.

And in the digital age, there's never been more information available to steer you to the exact right people whose problems you can solve. In fact there's so many ways to find out what you need to know, you need 80/20 just to sort out your information sources.

Selling to the *right* person is more important than all the sales methods, copywriting techniques, and negotiation tactics in the world. Because the *wrong* person doesn't have the money. Or the wrong person doesn't care. The wrong person won't be persuaded by anything.

This is not just about customers, either. It's about everything that makes money change hands: the product lines you choose to sell, the web pages you optimize, the PR opportunities you pursue. Offers, prices, and systems.

Books, scripts, headlines, guarantees, proposals, and risks. Employees, vendors, salespeople, managers, and government officials. 80/20 is already sifting them and sorting them, doing the hard work for you. Your job is to just pay attention. And rack that shotgun.

PARETO SUMMARY

▷ "Rack the shotgun" means triggering your audience and seeing who responds.

▷ Before you bet your time or money on any sales or business project, you need to rack the shotgun.

You Can Do Better

No matter who you are or what level of success you have achieved, invisible leverage points hide under the hood of your company and your career. For you right now, it is possible to work less and make more. Without a doubt. Most of the time, *much* more. Increases of 25 percent, often 250 percent, are not just possible but an everyday occurrence.

I spent most of my very first sales job pounding the phone, pounding the pavement, working the "numbers game." Every morning when I went to work, I flipped open the manufacturer's directory and trolled through the listings, making cold calls. I spent half to three-fourths of my day cold prospecting, trying to bust through doors and pry my way in to see buyers and decision-makers.

My life was a seesaw of filling my calendar with appointments (stomach-churning misery), going to my appointments (sometimes fun, seldom productive), then ending my week with the dreaded prospect of accosting more strangers again on Monday morning.

One day it occurred to me that most companies have an engineer named Dave. I'd call the switchboard and say, "Can I talk to Dave in Engineering?" The lady would say, "Dave Wilson?"

"Yeah, uh, Dave Wilson."

Ten seconds later I was paddling like crazy, trying to get "Dave Wilson" to lower his defenses and not hang up on me.

It took years of financial disaster, a near-nervous breakdown, and all kinds of frustration and rejection for me to finally recognize that I, and the company I worked for, were both defining my job the wrong way.

80 percent of that job was menial, low-level grunt work.

Not surprisingly, my pitches to "Dave in Engineering" tended to not be all that effective. If I'd spent 80 percent of my time in front of the right people, instead of not even knowing who to talk to, I would have instantly tripled my income.

During those two years, my efforts barely moved the needle. Seldom did I earn any commission above my base. With a wife and a new baby at home, we spiraled into debt and roiled with frustration.

About 18 months into that saga, I accidentally stumbled on direct marketing. What I found out was that if I focused my time and money on *racking the shotgun* and paying attention to whose head whipped around when they heard that sound instead of playing poker with every bloke who walked by, and if I steadfastly rejected the cold-calling game and insisted on finding other ways to sort people out, I reaped not one but two benefits: Not only did I spend far more time having actual conversations with qualified prospects, they *respected* me much more as well.

Suddenly I didn't have to get sleazy and manipulative to attract someone's attention. Quite the opposite, in fact. As I began to "rack the shotgun" instead of pounding the phone, my experience as a young sales guy transformed like magic.

I started a new job. In many ways it was similar to my old job but with one important difference. We'd designed our website to walk customers through a complex decision-making process and seeded the marketplace with user-friendly tools that positioned us as experts.

I would get emails from prospects trying to sort out their options and respond. I'd get on the phone, and eventually they'd give me their credit card or purchase order number.

I'll never forget my first sale. The customer was Micron, a company that makes semiconductor chips. With our help they'd figured out exactly how to apply our technology. After I got done talking to the engineer, the purchasing agent called me with a purchase order. Just like that.

Suddenly selling was . . . *easy*.

Each morning when I came to work, I found fresh leads on my desk—faxes, emails, voice mails, inquiries from magazines. Everyone I talked to *already wanted to talk to me.* I have not made a single cold call in 15 years.

I was only a wet-behind-the-ears, 29-year-old punk at that point. I hadn't even gotten *good* at direct marketing yet. But I had made one solid step into 80/20 living and thinking, without even realizing it. 80 percent of my time was now spent with the right people.

Fast forward 18 months . . . the web is coming on strong. I'm headed down the rabbit hole of online and offline advertising. The vast majority of businesses waste huge sums on ineffective advertising.

John Wanamaker famously said, "Half the money I spend on advertising is wasted; the trouble is I don't know which half." But Wanamaker was being optimistic. Most advertising is hugely wasteful. I know from experience, he wasn't wasting half; he was wasting 80 percent. Maybe more.

He didn't know how to take the 80 percent of money he was wasting and pour it into the right 20 percent. He didn't know his ROI wouldn't just improve by four times; it would improve 16 times. He was missing 96 percent of his opportunities.

As I laser-focused my efforts on prospects who already understood what we did, had problems we could solve, and believed in our way of solving them, I got far more results for my money than ever before. My first direct-mail campaign produced $8 of sales for every $1 we spent on postage and printing.

80/20 doesn't just apply to customers and billboards and mail drops. It applies to almost everything in business that you can count:

- 80 percent of the sales are made by 20 percent of the salespeople.

- A great album has 10 songs. Two of them make the pop charts, and one is a number-one hit.
- 80 percent of the customer service headaches come from 20 percent of the "problem children."
- 80 percent of warranty claims come from 20 percent of the product defects.
- 80 percent of the foot traffic walks through 20 percent of your store.
- 80 percent of your productivity comes from 20 percent of the tasks on your to-do list.
- 80 percent of the persuasion happens on 20 percent of your web pages.

And this is only the tip of the iceberg, because 80 percent of the 80 percent comes from 20 percent of the 20 percent. It's not just 80/20, but 80/20 squared and 80/20 cubed. 1000:1 leverage points are hiding all over the place.

But none of it is possible until you find someone to sell to. That's what we're going to talk about next.

PARETO SUMMARY

▷ 80/20 applies to almost everything in business that you can count.
▷ Almost every frustration you have in sales has something to do with ignoring 80/20.

4

80/20 Traffic
Where You Go to Get Customers

When I was a young, scrapping sales guy, I was trying to sell a new networking technology. It was hot and new and cutting edge (more like "bleeding edge"). I started going around to all kinds of companies in Chicago trying to sell it.

It wasn't terribly difficult to get appointments because a lot of people were curious. I would do "lunch and learns" and dog-and-pony shows at all kinds of companies.

But nobody ever bought anything.

One reason was this was a bleeding-edge product. There's an old saying: "Pioneers return with arrows in their backs." That was me. Any time you're in a situation like that, you have to be extra strategic. You can spend tons of money educating the public and never get a dime from anyone.

I would go to these companies and I would do these sales calls. A surprising amount of the time, I would see a little blue-and-white book on these guys' desks. This book was called *Understanding Device Level Networks,* and it was self-published by this company called Turck, who made a line of competing network components. Turck was my archenemy.

They would advertise their blue-and-white book and mail it out. It was a "lead generator." When they offered it in magazine ads and at trade shows, or even when their reps and distributors handed it out on site, whoever requested it was a lead. If not a hot prospect, they were at least lukewarm. Turck was *racking the shotgun.*

This had a nifty side benefit: It positioned them as authorities. They were the folks who "wrote the book." There were no other books on this subject at the time. Theirs was the only one.

Time after time, I would go back to a customer, they would thank me for coming in and filling in their knowledge gaps and tell me that they'd bought their new system from Turck.

I was trying to do missionary work: "I'm going to come in and I'm going to show you this networking technology and I'm going to show you how you hook it all up and show you how it works. I'm going to explain it aaaall to you."

Some of them would let me in and patiently listen while I explained it all—then they would go buy the stuff from Turck. *I was trying to be an authority, but I was knocking on their door in a way that positioned me as a beggar. You can't do that. It's just about impossible to close the sale.*

When you do publicity like writing books or magazine articles or blogging, the publicity itself will almost never close the deal for you. It will just move you to the front of the line. But you still have to get in the line. (Or better yet, make *them* get in *your* line.)

At minimum, you need a mechanism for turning the publicity into a sales funnel, like an offer of a white paper or diagnostic tool or problem-solving cheat sheet. A cheat sheet is a one-page document that super-summarizes a complex topic. Great cheat sheets are a lot of work to write because there's no room for filler. But that's exactly why people love them. Ditto with diagnostic tools—a handy example is my "Is Facebook for Me" tool at www.IsFBforMe.com.

Maybe you say, "Send an email to this special address and we'll send you the cheat sheet." Then there needs to be a next step and a next step. A conveyor belt that moves everything forward.

Turck was eating my lunch at the old company. But I learned my lesson fast, and when I went to a new company, we created a handy slide chart that compared 10 different technologies and offered it to anyone who wanted it. Engineers who were trying to make decisions found this thing very useful, and we gave away thousands.

One company even bought a case of 1000 charts (they paid 93 cents apiece for them) and gave them to all their sales reps at a national sales meeting. Not only were they advertising for us, they were paying for the privilege.

Pareto Point

Now I was operating on a different set of rules, and I was much more successful.

THE SEVEN CARDINAL RULES OF THE 80/20 SALES PRO

These are the seven cardinal rules of the 80/20 sales professional:

1. No cold calling. Ever. You should attempt to sell only to warm leads.
2. Before you try to sell anything, you must know how much you're willing to pay to get a new customer.
3. A prospect who "finds" you first is more likely to buy from you than if you find him.
4. You will dramatically enhance your credibility as a salesperson by authoring, speaking, and publishing quality information.
5. Generate leads with information about solving problems, not information about the product itself.
6. You can attain the best negotiating position with customers only when your marketing generates "deal flow" that exceeds your capacity.
7. The most valuable asset you can own is a well-maintained customer database, because people who've already bought from you are way easier to sell to than strangers.

I developed a great rule of thumb. I looked at all my customers and focused on my top 10 customers. The top 10 are the accounts that I'm paying attention to, trying to help them out, and ultimately trying to close business.

I decided, I'm going to take all of the magazine editors that are in my industry, and as a group they will get as much attention as one of my 10 best customers. This meant as a group, they got 3 percent to 5 percent of my time. I took their phone calls and returned their phone calls. I kept up with them and their editorial schedules, just like I kept up with my customers' buying schedules.

Building relationships with the press is not how most salespeople prioritize their time. A short-sighted sales manager or boss will typically pronounce that this is a waste, insisting that it's a "numbers game," and you just need to make more calls and drive more miles and see more people. He'll tell you you're lazy and trying to dodge doing your job. He'll be foolish for thinking that, as you'll see.

I made friends with those editors and offered to write them magazine articles. This strategy got over 100 pages of free publicity over a span of 18 months. That publicity cost nothing but time and shoe leather—zero dollars. In less than two years, we were *everywhere* in our tiny little industry. (Most industries are very small when you get right down to it. Before long, people from coast to coast know your name.)

Everyone knew who we were, and even though we only had 15 employees, we were taking on billion-dollar firms. The articles I wrote racked the shotgun, bringing us emails, leads, and phone calls from hot prospects.

That ended up being hugely beneficial for me personally, because when I left the company I realized, "Hey, wait a second. I've got good relationships with literally 10 different magazine editors in this industry, and the relationship is not with the company I work for, it's with me!"

This had happened almost by accident.

The editors didn't care what I sold, because they knew if they wanted a good article about something, they could come to me and I'd write it. So all I've got to do is find companies that want magazine articles written that will put a favorable slant on what they do, and I can sell advertising space.

Let's say a trade magazine ad cost $6,000 a page, which it did. I would say, "I'll write you a two-page article, and that's $12,000 worth

YOU GOTTA GET TRAFFIC

The first step to getting anyone to listen to you is getting ears and eyeballs. There's a huge range of media outlets you can use to get in front of people and/or acquire customers:

- Foot traffic and physical space in a retail store
- Radio: AM, FM, satellite
- Podcasts
- TV
- Google AdWords
- Ads in e-zines
- Endorsed email blasts from affiliates
- craigslist
- Pop-under and popup ads on other sites
- Postcard mailings
- Direct-mail letters
- Facebook ads
- Twitter
- LinkedIn ads
- Magalogs—catalogs that look like magazines
- Spots in other peoples' catalogs
- FedEx envelopes to highly targeted prospects from carefully selected mailing lists
- Banner ads
- YouTube videos
- Telemarketing
- Press releases
- Books
- eBay
- Yahoo! stores
- Amazon Kindle books

continued

YOU GOTTA GET TRAFFIC, CONTINUED

- Appearance as an "expert" on a talk show
- Exhibitions at trade shows
- Infomercials
- Free white papers
- Fliers distributed house to house or business to business
- A custom teleseminar for another person's email list
- Guest blogging
- Reverse auction sites like Elance.com
- Ads in magazines
- Pinterest
- Remnant space in local newspapers, purchased at deep discount rates
- Presentions at seminars
- Magazine articles and e-zine articles
- Flier inserts in newspapers, magazines, or mail-order shipments (that's called "insert media")
- "Dimensional Mail"–sending people interesting objects with a letter attached. (One guy I know mailed out a six-foot canoe paddle. Another stuck his note in a pouch stuck to a basketball. Another mailed an iPod Nano with a personally recorded message on the player.)

of space. But I'll only charge you $3,000 to write and place the article," which is exactly how I transitioned from a wage slave to an independent consultant—writing magazine articles.

This was because of the relationships I had with these editors. That's a good publicity strategy for any salesperson who doesn't mind sitting down and writing.

The best part is, through this strategy of generating leads, using publicity and positioning, not making cold calls, and selling to our hot leads, we grew that part of our business from $200,000 in sales to $4 million in four years. We sold the company to a publicly traded firm for $18 million.

As a marketer or salesperson, you MUST thoroughly master at least one form of advertising media. Until you do, you will be at the mercy of whatever comes along. You'll be cold-calling all day, or knocking on doors, or praying for rain, or hoping some guy in the marketing department does his job.

The Yin and Yang of Media and Traffic Expertise

The yin: It's impossible to become proficient in every form of advertising. You need to focus on one to three forms of marketing and advertising, so that you are much more skilled in the use of those media than most people.

The yang: If your entire business is dependent upon one source of traffic, one advertising medium, your business is a stool with only one leg. A train wreck waiting to happen. You need to get new customers from a diverse range of sources.

This yin and yang IS about balancing of specialty and diversity. Putting all your eggs in one basket is a lousy long-term plan. But spreading yourself too thin is just as bad.

Most direct- and online-marketing success stories I've seen over the last 10 years have this in common: The entrepreneur became extremely proficient at the use of ONE sales channel and used it to develop a firm foothold in a desperately competitive marketplace.

So the first thing you need to do as a marketer is master one of these. Make this your absolute, paramount, number-one priority. Then you can pick up another and start diversifying your business. I have an expanded report in the online supplement at www.perrymarshall.com/8020supplement that reviews the pros and cons of these various marketing channels.

Ultimately, the solution to the specialty/diversity problem is in the "winner take all" phenomenon which I explain in Chapter 10.

PARETO SUMMARY

▷ Cold calling is dead. You should talk only to prospects who are genuinely interested in what you have to sell.
▷ Don't use shoe leather and cold calling to generate leads. Think positioning, not prospecting.

▷ If your company won't generate sales leads for you, generate them yourself. Mastering at least one form of advertising media beats cold calling any day.

▷ There are many dozens of sources of advertising, publicity, and traffic. You *must* master at least one of them.

How to Use the "Invisible Money" Finder at www.8020Curve.com

N ow that I've covered the basics of 80/20 traffic, I'm going to show you how to *really* put 80/20 to work in a serious way, because so far I've only scratched the surface of how you can use it. Then in the chapters after that, I'll give you more high-power principles and techniques to add to your marketing toolbox.

But first, the simplest, most powerful business x-ray tool I've ever used: a website that makes 80/20 predictions.

Pareto
Point

Discover the 80/20 Power Curve—www.8020curve.com

When I first discovered the power of 80/20, I immediately pictured the Power Curve in my mind. But I hunted everywhere and couldn't find anything exactly like it, so I decided to create it myself.

This tool is a breakthrough that evolved over a long span of time. It's eerily accurate and applies to literally a million different things. For proof of that, or if you just enjoy numbers, flip to the Appendix and see how accurately this tool models a wide range of things from the sizes of Fortune 500 companies, to donations at a small church, to milk production in Wisconsin.

For several years it's been my secret weapon. I don't approach a single marketing problem without picturing this tool in my mind. Let's start using it now.

You've got 100 people, and you offered them a $50 product. 40 of them bought it. What does that look like? Plug the numbers into the tool like this:

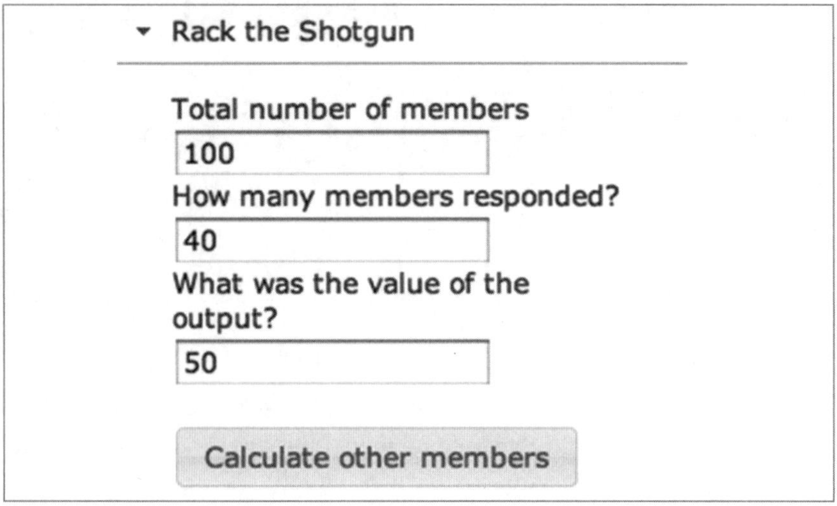

▼ **Rack the Shotgun**

Total number of members

| 100 |

How many members responded?

| 40 |

What was the value of the output?

| 50 |

[**Calculate other members**]

Figure 5–1.

Here's what the resulting Power Curve looks like, in Figure 5–2 on page 33.

The shaded area represents the money you've collected: 40 people x $50 = $2,000. The part above the shaded area shows you how much more money those people are *capable* of spending if you have more to offer them.

Since those 40 people bought a $50 product (assuming other people saw the offer and didn't respond), how many would buy a $30 product? The tool tells you. Enter the 30 in this box (shown in Figure 5–3, page 33).

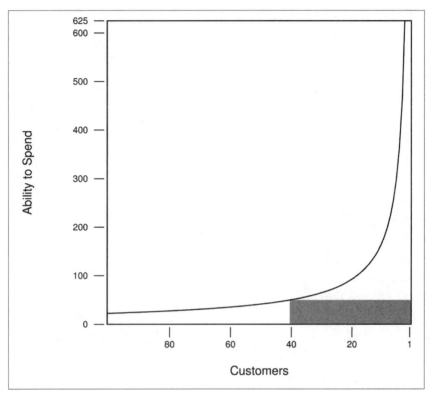

Figure 5–2.

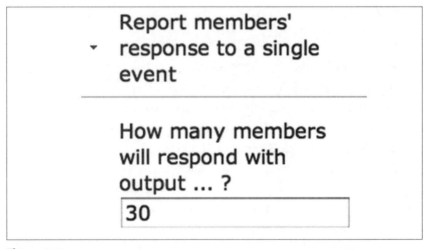

Figure 5–3.

And here's the curve, in Figure 5–4.

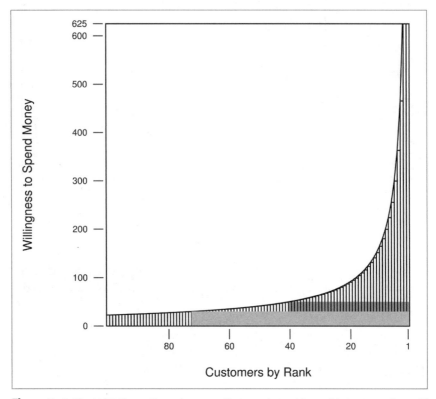

Figure 5–4. The 80/20 Power Curve shows you if 40 people would spend $50, 72 people would spend $30.

How many would buy a $200 product? See Figure 5–5 on page 35.

Answer: Eight would spring for a $200 product.

This requires that the more expensive product seem proportionally valuable to those people! The customers must feel the $200 product is worth it. They won't pay $200 for a $1.40 cup of coffee, but they will pay $200 for the espresso machine that went on sale today. So your job as a marketer is to offer them things that they consider to be worth greater amounts of money. If you don't offer them a super-deluxe experience, they'll buy one from somebody else.

One of your highest aspirations as a marketer should be becoming the alchemist who crafts endlessly irresistible offers, such that people spend a

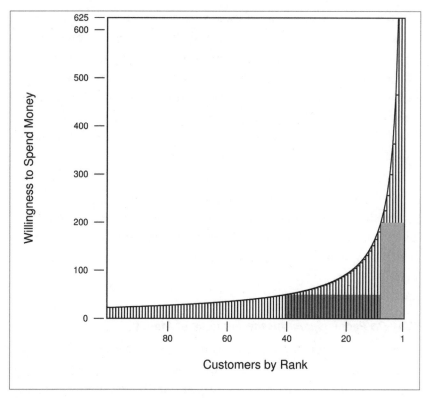

Figure 5–5. The curve also shows you if 40 people spent $50, 8 will spend $200.

disproportionate amount of money with you. Not only do they buy from you instead of anybody else, they spend far more buying your *kind* of thing than anyone might have ever expected.

That's what Starbucks did to coffee. They weren't merely better at coffee than the shop down the street—*they converted coffee into a luxury item.* Suddenly gourmet coffee took off like a rocket.

The 80/20 of Sports Fanatics

Sports teams harness a very special kind of feedback: sports fanatics' unscratchable itch. They do this with season tickets, skyboxes, and private clubs. If you want to see the Chicago Bears, you can get into a single game for as little as $19. Season tickets range from $1,000 for mediocre seats to $10,000 for the best seats near the 50-yard line.

But that's only the start of the luxury options, because season access to skyboxes costs tens of thousands of dollars and up, accommodating a dozen or two dozen people. The most luxurious skyboxes require multi-year commitments of hundreds of thousands of dollars. How do sports teams get 50 percent of their revenue from 1 percent of customers? *They scratch the unscratchable itch.*

Question: How much will a raving football fanatic, who has money, spend on football?

Answer: a virtually unlimited amount.

A few will spend a million dollars per year. They'll spend that money if someone offers them a complete, all-inclusive experience. They can be completely immersed in football, literally and figuratively. They can invite their friends and clients and know that everyone will be treated like foreign dignitaries.

Why Do People Spend Insane Amounts of Money?

Here's a little marketing secret for you: *Almost everybody has at least one passion, one interest, one obsession where they'll gleefully spend irrational amounts of money.* For some it's makeup or shoes. For some it's rock concerts. For some it's bowling. For some it's bird watching. For some it's skiing.

Even a very conservative, frugal 56-year-old gentleman, who drives a six-year-old Crown Victoria even though he can afford a top-of-the-line Mercedes. If he *really, really loves football,* he will buy a skybox. Somehow, he'll find a way to justify it.

The ultimate determiner is the simple fact that he has the money.

The Power Curve says that if 50,000 people will spend at least $100 per ticket for a football game, 238 will spend more than $10,000 (see Figure 5–6, page 37).

The curve on the right side goes up and up and up. It goes infinitely high and never quite touches the right side. The only limit on 80/20 is that there's a finite number of people. But if you had an infinite number of people, one of them would spend an infinite amount of money. (Yeah, I know. It's mind-bending.)

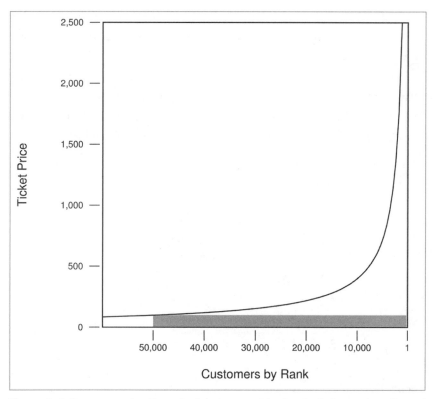

Figure 5–6. If 50,000 people will spend at least $100 per ticket for a football game, 238 will spend more than $10,000.

That's because 80/20 is *fractal*, which means it's a repeating pattern where the smallest parts resemble the whole. Consider your lungs. Each one of your lungs is about the size of your hand, but the interior surface area is the size of a football field. That's because the alveoli, the tiny cavities inside your lungs, are branches within branches within branches. Even though the surface of the lung is two-dimensional, its textured interior surface makes it nearly three-dimensional (2.97 to be exact). That makes the lung itself almost four-dimensional.

Lungs are exponentially more effective because of this. Businesses that exploit these laws of nature are, too. This book is about making your 3-D business 4-D.

Half the money in the sports industry comes from exploiting this amazing propensity for a tiny percentage of fans to spend outrageous amounts of money. But to get the full picture, we need to look in the other direction. What about the massive numbers of people who never even come to the game?

Using the exact same numbers, ask the tool: How much money will "fan number one million" spend? In other words, if we go way out to the left, to the *dis*interested people, how much money is available from them?

Punch this data into the 80/20 Power Curve as you see here:

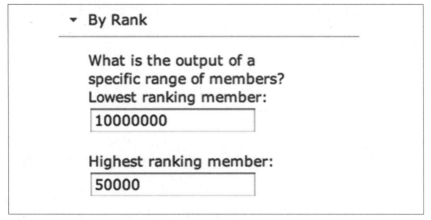

Figure 5–7.

Here's what it tells you: The one millionth most avid fan spent $7.57, and fan No. 50,000 spent $100.

What does that mean?

Remember, they didn't go to the game. But some people spent just as much money *not* going to the game as the ones who went. Can you spend money on football without going to the game? Absolutely. One of them watched the match at a sports bar. They were influenced by TV commercials. They bought shirts and shoes and hats and team-branded merchandise. They subscribed to pay-per-view. They rented videos of a past Superbowl game.

In fact, we can go out one step farther: members 10 million through 1 million.

Fan number one million spends $7.57. Fan number ten million spends $1.04. Maybe all he did was watch a few games, and $1.04 is how much advertising revenue they generated.

What about Fan number one at the far opposite extreme? I punch in "members 1 through 1" in "examine members by rank" and it says $1.1 million.

So, across 10 million people, the least interested fan spent a buck and the most interested fan spent $1.1 million. The tool says total revenue from all sources = $67,765,010. That's *per game.*

By the way, the least accurate portion of the Power Curve is the bottom left. I've found people at the bottom generally earn less and spend less than the curve predicts. That's because of "broken feedback loops." (I explain this further in the Appendix.) The tool assumes that everyone's at least a little bit interested in football, but some people hate it. Maybe fan number 10 million is worth only 10 cents. Fortunately, the non-football fans hardly matter at all, and the raving maniac fans matter a great deal.

Remember, at the beginning I assumed: This is a game where at least 50,000 people spent at least $100 per ticket. If this is an above-average game, and other games were less popular, then we would guess that the Chicago Bears' total revenue is a few hundred million bucks.

Is that correct?

According to Forbes, the Bears' total revenue for 2010 was $266 million with gate receipts of $61 million. Yes, those numbers fit pretty nicely with mine.

With just one piece of information—the least expensive ticket on a popular game day—the Power Curve gives you a surprisingly accurate estimate of the entire economic picture of a sports team with millions of fans, from 11-year-old kids to billionaires with luxury skyboxes.

Why? Because 80/20 isn't just a business rule of thumb. It's a law of nature.

This only scratches the surface of all the things you can do with this tool. You can put the numbers for almost anything you can measure into the tool, and it will tell you something you didn't know before. I recommend you check the Appendix to find out more.

A lot of sports are characterized by this kind of hyper-responsive behavior. Golfers are notorious for being maniacs, and I know a lot of marketers who've made fortunes selling golf products. Wherever there are rabid, obsessive customers, there's a great business.

But 80/20 doesn't apply to everything. For example, "number of kids in a family" doesn't follow the 80/20 rule. That's because for most people, having one kid doesn't necessarily make you want to have a second kid even more. By the time most people get to three to four kids, their lives have grown sufficiently complex. Families of eight kids are fairly rare.

But it is present in most places. If you have a church of 400 people, 50 percent of the work gets done by 1 percent of the people—probably four paid staff members. Almost all the volunteering gets done by less than 100 people. The least active 300 people in the church do next to nothing, other than maybe showing up on Sunday.

If you have 400 people and they're all actively participating, your attendance ain't gonna stay at 400 for long! It's going to grow. This is true in any volunteer organization—church, charity, Meetup group, or parent-teacher association.

Have you ever noticed that out of Jesus' 12 apostles, three were extra-special disciples? Peter, James, and John. The 12 were chosen from a group of 70. 80/20 is everywhere you look, even there. The bad road is wide and the good road is narrow. *You cannot change this. All you can do is decide whether you're going to let it work* for *you or* against *you.*

Even though you can't change the 80/20 Power Curve, you can raise the excitement level and participation of everyone in your organization. Whether we're talking about churches, schools, charities, or standards committees, some are hotbeds of activity and others are tombs. Why? Because the speed of the leader determines the speed of the pack.

When the leader raises the intensity level, the organization grows. 80/20 is still in force, but you've attracted more people and the top performers do more.

80/20 Works the Same Whether You're Looking at 10 People or a Billion

The shape of the 80/20 Power Curve never changes much. Whether we're looking at the incomes of all seven billion people in the world, or the wages of shoe salesmen in Kuala Lumpur, or the Forbes 400, or the 10 richest people in the world, the Power Curve remains the same. (I've included a bonus section on the Power Curve in the Appendix. If you like numbers, make sure you take a look.)

This means that your job is to climb the Power Curve from wherever you are right now, moving time and energy from the left to the right. It means that as you move to the right, bigger opportunities will appear in front of you.

PARETO SUMMARY

▷ The 80/20 Power Curve is the most important chart in any business.

▷ The Power Curve is true whether you're looking at 10 people or 10 billion.

▷ You can punch what you know into www.8020curve.com, and it will either report a bunch of other numbers that *are* true in your business or else *will be true* once you've maximized every opportunity.

▷ Your top job as an 80/20 marketing professional is to move resources from the left to the right.

Simplify Your Life with the Power Triangle

There are three steps to selling anything.

The first step is getting **traffic**: You gotta get human bodies, eyes, and ears, to sell to—without raising their defenses, if at all humanly possible.

The next step is **conversion**: You have to convince the person that what you have is going to solve their problem.

The final step is **economics**: You have to give them something that's valuable and get their money.

Traffic, conversion, and economics form a **Power Triangle** that governs everything that happens in sales and marketing.

You should always be suspicious of complicated things. You should be even more suspicious of people who make simple things complicated.

The beautiful thing about the Power Triangle is how simple it is. Einstein knew he was onto something big with a simple equation:

$$e = mc^2$$

Even a seventh-grader can deal with that, with a little help from his science teacher.

Things that are *true* and *correct* tend to have that sort of simplicity.

Which brings me to the Power Triangle, a brainchild of my marketing manager, Jack Born. The Power Triangle, in Figure 6–1, always takes you where you need to go, and the 80/20 in the center always focuses you on the points of highest effectiveness. It's a work of genius.

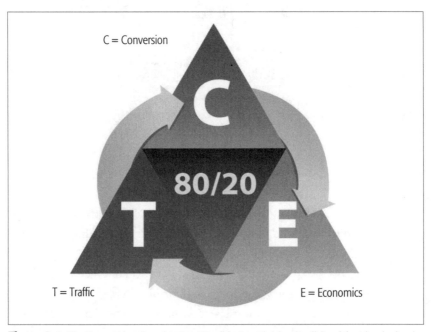

Figure 6–1. The Power Triangle and 80/20. Warning: Don't let the simplicity of the triangle deceive you. You can do many things with this tool. (Illustration by Danielle Flanagan.)

In order to sell something, you have to get **Traffic**; then you have to **Convert** the traffic. **Economics** means you have to make some money on what you sell. That's why you're in business.

When you make a profit you can re-invest it in getting more **Traffic** and **Converting** the traffic and further improving your **Economics**. And so it goes, clockwise in a circle. It's a spiral of never-ending Traffic, Conversion, and Economics.

That's the essence of marketing. It describes *every* human transaction. You can apply it to romance or volunteering for the Peace Corps or trading favors with your fishing buddies.

Figure 6–2. 80/20 is multi-layered: There's an 80/20 inside each 80/20. (Illustration by Danielle Flanagan.)

The first thing to notice about the Power Triangle is the 80/20 principle sits at the center. It's there for a good reason.

80/20 is in the center because everything revolves around getting more out for putting less in. And finally, 80/20 is fractal. Inside every top 20 percent is another top 20 percent.

Let the Power Triangle Work for You

You come to me and say, "I've developed this cool new invention, and it's going to make millions of dollars. How do I sell it?"

We're instantly in Marketing 101. Before we begin some lengthy talk about buying clicks or writing emails or infomercials or any other technique, you need to answer four questions:

1. *Who* would buy this? (that's **T**)
2. What can we say to *persuade* them to buy? (that's **C**)
3. Can you reach them *affordably*? (that's **E**)
4. Can they *give* you money? (that's **E**)

The second thing I want you to notice about the Triangle is: **You needed to go *counterclockwise* to decide how to sell something.**

Which means the primary skill you must master in marketing is ***thinking backward.***

When I was a young-pup marketer writing sales copy, I would remind myself: *Perry, you're not **you**, you're **them**. In your imagination, you're not sitting at **your** computer anymore; you're sitting at **theirs**. You're not interested in what **you're** interested in; you're interested in what **they're** interested in.* I pictured myself physically doing a 180.

I do that exercise every time I sell anything. It's become second nature.

To build a sales funnel, you *begin with the end in mind*, to use Stephen Covey's famous words. You start from the end, and you work your way to the beginning.

Figure 6–3. The Sierpinski Triangle fits an infinite number of triangles into finite space. The Power Triangle is similar.

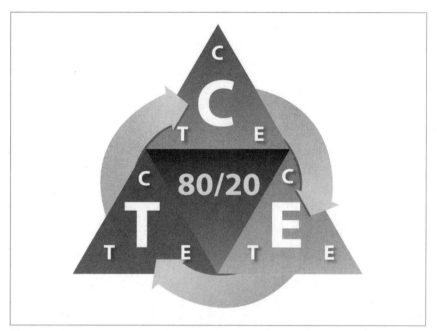

Figure 6–4. Zoom in, zoom out, the Triangle is the same. Each element always contains all three elements. (Illustration by Danielle Flanagan.)

Then traffic comes into the funnel at the beginning and goes clockwise to the economic end.

But since selling starts with traffic, *advanced* marketers don't begin with the invention (i.e., the final transaction). We begin by asking ourselves: "What would these people want to buy?" Then we create it or find it.

You should also see that there's a Power Triangle inside each element of the Triangle.

It's true on every scale (demonstrated in Figure 6–4). Zoom in, zoom out, it's still there. It's true on the micro level, and it's true on the macro level. Let's say that your traffic is Google ads, your conversion is a website sales page, and your economics is that you sell shoes.

Inside those Google ads we find another Triangle, as shown in Figure 6–5, page 48.

Let's say your visitors land on a page that offers a white paper in exchange for name, company, snail mail, and email address. There's a Power Triangle there, too:

Figure 6–5. Traffic = People who see the ad; Conversion = Ad copy; Economics = Clicks and cost per click. (Illustration by Danielle Flanagan.)

- **Traffic = People who land on your page**
- **Conversion = People who opt in and the reasons they did.** They want the cheat sheet or price quote; they want to take the quiz, or they want the free software download.
- **Economics = What they get in exchange for their email address and the value of that address to you**

The *economic value* of an email address is huge. Even with social media, blogs, Twitter, and everything else, email is still the center of the marketing universe. The number-one function of your website is to collect an email address from your visitor before he leaves.

And there's still an 80/20 inside the Google ad: Three to four words in your ad swing most of the response. The most influential element is the offer made in your ad.

Your visitor buys a pair of shoes at your retail store. There's a Power Triangle there, too:

- **Traffic = People who came into the shoe store**
- **Conversion = Emotional and practical benefits of buying the shoes**

Figure 6–6. Inside your sales funnel, conversion still involves Traffic, Conversion, and Economics. (Illustration by Danielle Flanagan.)

- **Economics = What they paid for the shoes**

You send an email to your email list.

- **Traffic = People who get the email**
- **Conversion = Those who do what the email asks of them and the benefits to them, even if it's not an actual purchase—it could be watching a video**
- **Economics = WHY they respond and the benefit to you**

Someone clicks on a Google ad (traffic) and lands on your opt-in page (conversion) and gives you their email address (economics). Later you send them an email (traffic), and now they're on your sales page (conversion) and you're asking them to buy something (economics).

Every move you make comes down to:

- Stimulus
- Response

- Payoff

Great marketers and sales gurus have said **Traffic + Conversion = Profits**, and it's true, but it's incomplete.

Economics speaks to the importance of value, and as you consider this, you'll see it's really the most important thing of *all*. Economics drives everything else.

This Means

- The core essence of marketing is how much you are willing to pay to acquire a customer. How well you compete comes down to how much you can afford to pay. That's economics.
- It's all math and psychology. Much attention is given to psychology, but math is absolutely critical. Good math can save mediocre persuasion, but bad math will sink the best sales pitch every time.

During most of my consultations, economics is the *first* thing I seek to improve. *Begin with the end in mind.* Make every transaction more valuable.

Capitalize on the willingness of the top-shelf customer to spend money. Do upsells and cross-sells and sell 'em something else. *Sell results, not procedures.* In other words, don't just sell "pieces parts" and components and items on an *a la carte* menu. Sell complete packages that simply and elegantly solve the total problem with as little fuss as possible.

Create new offerings and new experiences. Invent new products. Imagine what your customers would happily part money for.

Get More Traffic and More People to Sell to, NOW

Next we apply this—and 80/20—to traffic sources.

Most people don't realize the vast range of options you have when you rent and buy snail mail lists, email lists, and phone lists. There are two kinds of lists:

1. *Compiled lists*: For example, "All the dental offices in the United States," or "All the households in zip code 68505," or "All males between ages 31 and 40 in Cook County, Illinois."

2. *Response lists*: For example "Everyone who subscribed to *Black Belt* magazine in the last 90 days," or "People who donated over $100 to the Sierra Club in the last two years," or "People who bought items from the Hammacher Schlemmer gadget catalog."

Compiled lists are things you know about groups of people, generally based on publicly available information. A compiled list is w-a-a-a-y better than just calling names out of a phone book. (I actually did that for a time. It was brutal.)

You can easily get a compiled list of "SIC codes," four-digit numbers that the U.S. government uses to categorize businesses. SIC stands for "Standard Industry Classification." If you sell any kind of stationery, you could get a list of all companies in SIC code 5943, for stationery stores, and you're going to have a way easier job.

Compiled lists are usually sold. You might pay one cent to a dollar per name for a compiled list, depending on how sophisticated the information is and how many "selects" you buy. Often you can be very selective: "I want vice presidents or production managers, and I want companies with more than $10 million in revenue, who manufacture automotive parts." Once you buy a compiled list, you can use the data as long as you want to.

The problem with a compiled list is, it's just a list. It's way better than no list at all, but a lot of names on that list are very low quality because nobody's racked the shotgun.

Response lists are lists where someone *has* racked the shotgun. The reason someone is on the list is because he has bought something, subscribed to something, donated money, or gone to a trade show.

Response lists are much more valuable than compiled lists. And much more expensive. A compiled list—"Everyone who requested a free subscription to *Control Engineering* trade magazine in the last year"—adds a couple *more* layers of 80/20. A response list comes from someone who has already sorted through the world and gotten people to actually raise their hands. That usually means they've spent money.

Response lists typically cost anywhere from 10 cents to several dollars per name. In the mailing list world, "hotline" names are sold at a premium price. Hotline names are people who bought or subscribed within the last 90 days. That adds an extra 80/20 because if they made that purchase recently it means they're "in heat" and will probably respond to other, similar offers.

Suppose you have a miserable, cold-calling sales job. The fastest way to make your life w-a-a-y easier is to start renting or buying lists so that you are at least eliminating 90 to 99 percent of the time wasters. You'll discover that when you purchase information like this, you suddenly have a much clearer picture of who you're talking to and what you need to say to them.

It Is to Your Advantage to Pay for Quality!

Whether you're buying web traffic, making cold calls, sending out emails, mailers, or faxes, success starts with your list. If you get a cheap list and then spend all kinds of postage money sending mail to people who will never respond, that's dumb. Better to spend $2 per name and mail 500 letters to targeted prospects than get a "deal" paying 30 cents per name and mailing 5,000 letters to people who don't care.

If it costs $1 to mail your letter, here's how the economics work out. Let's say a response equals a $100 purchase.

> *High-quality list*: You mail to 500 people and get 30 to respond. $2 per name list rental + $1 postage x 500 = $1,500 cost. Revenue = $3,000 and you make $1,500 gross profit.
>
> *Low-quality list*: You mail to 5,000 people and get 40 to respond. $0.30 per name list rental + $1 x 5,000 = $6,500 cost. Revenue = $4,000, so you just lost $2,500 before you even covered your product cost. (By the way, I'm making the generous assumption that those same 500 good buyers are mixed in this 5,000-name list. *Not* always the case. Sometimes a low-quality list is pure junk.)

Sales is a *dis*qualification process! The more junk you can eliminate before you spend money and effort, the more effective you are. I'm going to address this in the next chapter.

Where to Get Lists

The most famous source of mailing lists in the United States is SRDS, the Standard Rate and Data Service, www.SRDS.com. SRDS is an online subscription service. There are thousands of list brokers that you can work through. Other sources you should investigate include Acxiom's List Direct, www.iblistdirect.com/. I also suggest exploring www.nextmark.com and www.Hoovers.com.

I buy lists from Ben Morris at Kristalytics (www.Kristalytics.com/list-brokering) who accesses 150 million household records with over 1,000 data points per record, which are combined from a variety of sources.

As soon as you have enough traffic to do an experiment, you need to focus on conversion. That's next.

PARETO SUMMARY

▷ Everything in sales and marketing is summed up in the Power Triangle: traffic, conversion, economics, and 80/20.

▷ Traffic comes first, then conversion, then economics. But great marketers think backwards, which means starting with economics.

▷ There are two sides to economics: the money you get, and the value customers get in exchange for their money.

▷ The simplest, easiest way to get leads is to buy or rent a list. The quality of lists obeys 80/20—most are lousy; a small fraction are great.

▷ The most valuable asset you own is the customer list you build yourself.

7

80/20 Conversion
Now That You've Racked the Shotgun, Make 'Em MOVE

After four years of working the Vegas strip as a professional gambler, John Paul Mendocha was sitting in a restaurant booth with a couple of his gambling buddies. The other two were having an argument:

"Yes, you will."

"No, I won't."

"Yes, you will."

"No, I won't."

Out came a Glock. The guy planted the barrel on the other guy's skull.

"Yes, you WILL."

Suddenly John was having another "rack the shotgun" experience. This time, it wasn't an insight about who to play poker with. It was an insight about what kind of *hombres* he shouldn't be hanging with anymore. John said to himself, "Self, if you don't exit this business real soon, your sad little carcass is gonna wind up in a ditch somewhere."

So literally one day on a Tuesday afternoon, he walked away from the seedy world of gambling forever. He decided to get a real job. John had moved on.

Fast-forward a year or two, and John's working for a high-tech company in southern California. John's experience in all those casinos and dives has taught him a great deal about 80/20, and he understands it far better than his sales managers.

His sales manager hands him a stack of leads. "John, I want you to get appointments with all 206 of these people."

John knows that's ridiculous. John knows that 80 percent of those 206 are a complete waste of energy, and only about 4 percent are strong candidates. He just needs to find a way to find out who's worth his time.

So John devised one. It's called The Five Power Disqualifiers®.*

John's 206 leads were his **traffic**. His next challenge was **conversion:** What do you say to someone to convince them you can solve their problem?

At this point, most books would dive right into persuasion and salesmanship.

That would be a mistake.

That's because an 80/20 sales and marketing maven knows, even after you've stimulated interest and positioned yourself properly, there's still another step you need to make *before you try to convince anybody of anything.*

That step is: You must DISQUALIFY people who don't fit.

If they don't have the money, or your solution doesn't fit, or if there's no urgency, then there ain't going to be no sale.

John knew that out of 206 cold to lukewarm sales leads, fewer than 5 percent—probably no more than 10—were actually worth a face-to-face meeting and less than half of those would actually buy. If he called all 206

---

* The Five Power Disqualifiers® is a registered trademark of Speed Selling Inc. and used under license.

and asked them the right questions, he could save himself a huge amount of time, then spend the rest of his time delivering exactly what the real customers wanted.

The Five Power Disqualifiers®

Pareto Point

John reduced the sales process to five essential requirements that are *always* present when a sale is made. I know of no one else who has distilled sales and marketing to such a small number of fundamentals.

These go hand in hand with the Power Triangle, because these five things define the *who* of the traffic that you're trying to buy.

1. *Do they have the money?* Some markets consist of people who have no money. Sometimes the very market itself is defined as a herd of moneyless people. Doesn't mean you can't make a buck selling rent-to-own furniture, but know ahead of time it's going to be tricky to get blood out of them stones. People who do have the money are way easier to sell to!

2. *Do they have a bleeding neck?* A bleeding neck is a dire sense of urgency, an immediate problem that demands to be solved. Right. Now. If you want to make the big bucks, your product has to deal with something that involves one or both of the following: a) Pain and great inconvenience, loss of money, threat of loss, and/or b) some craving for pleasure that borders on the irrational. Big pain, big pleasure. Stuff that hits really close to the jugular or pocketbook. Serious money is always found in those places. If you want the check tomorrow, the problem today needs to be u-r-g-e-n-t.

   And before you ease the pain, you gotta intensify it.

   The guy says to you, "It hurts really bad, right here." You point to his elbow and say "You mean here?" and you smack his elbow with a hammer, hard. He yelps and sees stars for a moment. He nods and takes a big gulp, choking back tears.

   Yup. *Good market for you to go into.* What's the biggest, nastiest problem you've ever solved in your life? That's a real good start, right there.

3. *Do they buy into your unique selling proposition?* If you're just going into a market, the question is, what big benefit will they buy into? What kind of deal would they snatch up in a hot second? What benefit do they want that the other guys are not promising?

A unique selling proposition (USP) is your unique answer to these questions:

- What does your product do that nobody else's product does?
- Why should I buy from you instead of anybody else?
- What guarantee can you make that nobody else can make?

Your unique selling proposition is hugely important, and I will focus on it in much more detail in the next chapter. But for now, know that one of your most important jobs as a salesperson or marketer is to not only know the answers to these questions but constantly improve the USP of whatever you sell.

4. *Do they have the ability to say YES?* I've got a friend who lost a big bundle trying to sell a seminar to doctors. They had the money, they bought into his USP, they had a bleeding neck—most doctors were expressing grave dissatisfaction about financial matters that the seminar directly addressed—but it was almost impossible to get a piece of mail into any doctor's hands. Docs have their staff sort all their mail, and what Helga their assistant thinks is a bleeding-neck issue and what actually makes the doc's neck bleed? Two different things.

Helga the receptionist can say no, but she can't say yes. This is a huge problem when you're selling anything. Are you selling to an engineer who's going to have to get approval from his boss? Are you applying for a job through the human resources department—knowing that HR can only say no and only the VP can say yes?

(Hint: Never send resumes to HR. Find out who the hiring manager is, and send it to that person. Preferably in a hand-addressed #10 envelope with a stamp. I've included a special report on job hunting for salespeople in the online supplement, www.perrymarshall .com/8020supplement/.)

5. *Does what you sell fit in with their overall plans?* If your service requires major brain surgery on the part of the customer, he ain't

gonna take your offer unless brain surgery is literally a lot less painful than the alternative (e.g., dying). Whatever you sell needs to harmonize with natural, existing forces—both on the inside and outside of your prospect's world.

The most important thing John Paul will tell you about the Five Power Disqualifiers is you want to plow through them as fast as humanly possible.

Sales is, first and foremost, a *dis*qualification process, not a "convincing people" process! Step past the sick and the lame early in the game, and deal only with the healthy ones left standing. You will save yourself so much time.

The Five Power Disqualifiers are exhibit "A" of 80/20 thinking. In fact, each one typically gets rid of the bottom 80 percent of whomever you're dealing with. When you're honest with yourself about all five of these things, you're automatically dealing with the tippy-top of the pyramid— less than 1 percent.

Test Fast. Fail Fast. Move On. Next, Next, Next

So John used the Five Power Disqualifiers on his prospects and met only with the ones who passed all five tests. These companies were defense contractors, and he attracted them by explaining that everything his company shipped came with iron-clad guarantees of price, delivery, and performance parameters. Since the level of performance John promised greatly exceeded industry norms, his customers were extremely curious.

But his customers had to qualify by reciprocating with equal commitments.

Buyers were always intrigued by this, so many times they would meet John on *his* terms. Instead of driving to their facilities, he developed a different strategy.

He would set up camp at a restaurant booth, hand the waitress a $50 bill, and schedule meetings—one engineer or buyer per 90-minute slot— all day. One after another, bam-bam-bam.

So instead of driving all over southern California for eight weeks attempting to meet with 206 reluctant, skeptical prospects, he'd knock out a dozen meetings in a couple of days, seeing only the ones who were hot and ready to go.

And that's how John busted the ceiling on sales quota after sales quota, easily clearing $200,000 per year. Two hundred grand was serious coin in 1985.

Next: Give 'Em Your USP

If you're talking to your prospect on the phone, you need to start with a unique selling proposition that really gets his attention. This is NOT a good opener:

"Hi, this is Marty. I'm with Northwestern Mutual, and we've got $16.2 billion in assets under management."

Let me share a simple acid test that uses 80/20 to identify good headlines: Imagine you're writing a classified ad, and you're going to use your opening statement or headline in the ad copy:

I'm with Northwestern Mutual, and we've got $16.2 billion in assets under management. Marty, (800) 555-1212.

Woo-hoo, isn't that exciting? I can't wait to buy some insurance now.

Remember that all good sales copy is about your customer, not you. Good copy speaks to the bleeding neck first. Try this:

DANGER: If your net worth exceeds even a paltry $350,000, Nancy Pelosi is about to claw $50,000 from your bank account. Transcript from secret congressional committee. Marty (800) 555-1212.

Look at how many Power Disqualifiers we managed to use here: Money ($350,000); Bleeding Neck ("Pelosi is about to claw $50,000 from your bank account"); USP ("transcript from secret congressional committee"—nobody else is offering that). We crammed three out of the five into a couple of sentences.

A phone script might be, "Hi, this is Marty from Northwestern Mutual. You don't know me, but I just got my hands on a transcript from one of Nancy Pelosi's secret congressional committee meetings. If your net worth exceeds even 350K, she's gonna grab fifty grand fast. I can email this thing to you. Dude, this is really scary."

We're zeroing in on emotional hot buttons and getting straight to the point. No blathering or corporate MBA-speak.

Case Study of a Successful B2B Sales Message

Below is a hunk of copy I've used on my website. It's generated consistent leads every day for years. This is from www.perrymarshall.com/gm. I've highlighted the 20 percent that contains the key persuasion elements:

"Stop Cold-Calling Business Prospects, Battling Voice Mail—and Make Them Chase You Instead!"

Headline starts with their bleeding neck, then offers a benefit statement.

Dear Sales Professional,

After years of dialing for dollars, knocking on doors, and enduring all kinds of rejection and drudgery, I finally made a revolutionary discovery: You can cause the world to beat a path to your door. You can be an invited guest instead of an unwelcome pest. You don't call them—they call you.

The surest way to emotionally connect with a customer is to empathize with them, show them that a page of your diary looks an awful lot like their diary.

How does this happen? With the power of information and publicity and the science of results-accountable marketing.

From Failure to Success...

The results were nothing less than astonishing. I multiplied product sales by 2,000 percent, nearly tripled my income, and went from making hundreds of cold calls every month to nearly zero.

Most of this page is about pain and suffering, but I've deliberately thrown in some pleasure.

I helped grow a company from quasi-startup and no name recognition to over 100 pages of press exposure. Four years after I began, that business was acquired by a publicly traded company for 18 million dollars.

If you're making even ONE cold call a day, you're wasting time and money. And if your company is like 99 percent of all other businesses in America, you are ignoring millions of dollars in untapped sales.

A finely tuned marketing and publicity system delivers a predictable number of quality sales leads to you every day, month in and month out, so your salespeople spend time only with people who already understand what you do and who have proactively asked you to help them solve their problem.

Find their sore spot, and bang it with a hammer.

Has your medical doctor ever called you on the phone during dinnertime, asking if you might need help fighting a flu bug? I don't think so. He doesn't find you, you find him. And when you do see him, he tells you what medicine you need to take and you take it.

If he says you need surgery, you might seek a second opinion, but you're willing to pay good money for that opinion. And most likely you take the advice, no matter how painful or inconvenient.

Do Your Customers Respect You as Much as They Respect Their Doctor?

Ouch. More pain.

No? Why not? They don't know him any better than they know you. You went to school. You have expertise. You know how to solve difficult problems. So what's the difference?

The difference is *positioning*. The doctor is perceived to be an expert, so you seek his counsel. The medical industry knows things about marketing and positioning that most people in our industry just don't know. Most companies just imitate their competitors, and everyone gets dumber every year.

Headlines, italics, highlights and bolds emphasize the most important 20 percent for people who are skimming. This is called "Dual Readership Path."

I went on a mission to study the most brilliant minds in marketing today, across dozens of industries and professions. The system I've developed over the last five years delivers powerful results for corporate salespeople, in a measurable and predictable way. I now produce training tools and consult with a select number of high-tech clients.

Your experience as a business owner, marketing manager, or salesperson can radically change for the better in only a few month's time, simply by learning my system. I invite you to explore my website, and request my FREE Audio CD, *Guerrilla Marketing for Hi-Tech Sales People*. (All you cover is S&H.) It delivers 12 powerful bullets that bring cold-calling drudgery and advertising waste to an end.

Just fill out the contact form, and my capable staff will make sure you get it right away.

Sincerely,

Perry S. Marshall

P.S. You're probably thinking, "OK, so why is this guy giving away an *audiobook*? Is it any good, or is it just a shameless sales pitch?"

> Big promise, big benefit. Does getting more respect fit into their overall plans? Probably so!

> "Do they have the money?" Charging a few bucks for shipping and handling eliminated lots of tire-kickers, but interestingly, didn't eliminate buyers.

There are several reasons why I'm giving this away:

1. There are *lots* of salespeople, maybe you—who wake up every morning and think "Oh, yuck . . . I've got to get on the phone today, stay out of voice mail jail, and set up a bunch of appointments . . . . It's going to be a real grind." That's exactly how it was for me. Oh, to have only had this CD 10 years ago!

> More bleeding neck.

2. *In most companies, there is almost NO relationship between the marketing dollars that go out and the sales dollars that come in.* They spend a pile of money on advertising, and they don't know what they're getting for it. Then they start flogging the salespeople on the 26th of every month. This CD will show you how to fix that problem.

> Let's hammer on that sore spot some more. More pain.

3. Of course nobody's going to hire a consultant or invest money in sales tools unless they're convinced that I really know what I'm talking about. Listen to the CD and decide for yourself.

> This is no infomercial—it's solid information that you can use right away. I have a hunch you'll not only enjoy it but you'll probably pass it along to three to four other people, as others have done.
>
> <u>Fill out this form</u> to request a free copy of *Guerrilla Marketing for Hi-Tech Sales People.* (You just cover Shipping & Handling.)
>
> I promise you'll never think about sales the same way again!

Every sales message needs a call to action!

This Guerilla Marketing CD offer is a classic, decade-long lead generation success story. It employs my favorite persuasion formula, Problem—Agitate—Solve, which you see here in the copy that promotes it. You can make similar offers in thousands of different markets, and as long as you're *reading people a page in their own diary* and *speaking to them about the most painful things in their life,* you're racking the shotgun.

For a much deeper look at crafting sales messages and writing persuasive copy, listen to my interview with world-class copywriter John Carlton at www.perrymarshall.com/8020supplement.

PARETO SUMMARY

▷ *The Five Power Disqualifiers® are:*

1. Do they have the money?
2. Do they have a bleeding neck—an urgent problem that must be solved now?
3. Do they buy into your unique selling proposition?
4. Do they have the ability to say YES?
5. Does what you sell fit in with their overall plans?

▷ *Headline test:* If your headline were a classified ad, would it make the phone ring? Don't focus on your product. Focus on the urgent problem, the bleeding neck.

▷ *Best sales formula ever:* Problem—Agitate—Solve. Most people don't spend nearly enough time on the "Agitate" part.

8

Your USP
Unique Selling Proposition

Why should I buy from you right now, instead of buying anything else from anybody else next week?

What can you uniquely guarantee?

That's your USP.

If you have a great answer to that question, you can charge more money, have fatter margins, put more money into marketing and advertising, invest more in customer satisfaction and developing new products.

If you have a lousy answer to that question, you're in trouble before you even start.

Symptoms of a bad USP: You're constantly fighting downward price pressure. You battle directly with other people on price and delivery. You feel competitors breathing down your neck. The cost of advertising seems out of reach. You feel defensive about taking up customers' time. Nobody really wants to talk to you. You have to knock on lots of doors.

If that sounds like you, then there is something you're not promising, something you're not guaranteeing or not articulating specifically enough that's keeping you from being unique and keeping you from making more sales.

The pithiest USP I've ever seen—this has been running in *National Enquirer* for about six decades (!): "Corns gone in 5 days or money back."

That simple ad offers a crystal-clear solution to a problem, a specific amount of time, and an "or else" statement.

Domino's Pizza has one of the best-known USPs ever: A fresh, hot pizza delivered in 30 minutes or less, guaranteed. That's not unusual now, but in the 1970s, it was a blockbuster.

Four Questions Your USP Can and Should Answer

1. Why should I listen to you?

WHAT CAN YOU "MAKE" UNIQUE ABOUT YOU?

1. *Service*. Guaranteed friendliness. Guaranteed delivery. Guaranteed live person on the phone, etc.

2. *The market you serve is unique*, e.g., your focus is businesses with 10 employees or fewer.

3. *Your product is unique*. It has a guaranteed result. It's tailor-made for X kind of person. Using it is a guaranteed "experience."

4. *Your whole "experience" is unique*. A cab/limo driver promises hot Starbucks coffee and a morning newspaper waiting for you, and he'll have you to the airport on time or you don't pay.

5. *Your price is unique*. It may be a low price ("We'll beat anyone's advertised price or your mattress is free!"). It may carry a premium price (see the "Expensive . . . by Design" ad in Robert B. Cialdini's book, *Influence: The Psychology of Persuasion*). There are guaranteed add-ons that other competitors don't offer at your price (or which let you ask a higher price).

---

2. Why should I do business with you instead of anybody and every-body else?

3. What can your product do for me that no other product can do?

4. What can you guarantee me that nobody else can guarantee?

You can download a handy three-page USP worksheet and watch a presentation by the president of my company, Bryan Todd, at www.perrymarshall.com/8020supplement/**.**

Business vs. Personal USP; Current vs. Natural USP

What's your natural USP? So far we've been talking about the USP of your company, your product, or your service. If you sell 1,000 products, each product should have its own USP. But you also have a *personal* unique sell-ing proposition that stands distinct from your current product or business. It's the inherent groove based on your passion, personality, and experiences that you carry with you at all times.

Most people are only vaguely aware of their natural, personal USP. I think one of the biggest wormholes that people get sucked into is, they get so enamored with the romantic version of what somebody else does, the greener pastures, that they ignore the unromantic, plain, everyday genius that they themselves possess.

The thing I dislike MOST about being a marketing advisor is that it's so much harder to get people to focus on their own innate giftedness and natural USP.

It's easier to show people a bright shiny object and manipulate them into jumping on the next short-lived bandwagon than to master something that's just beginning to flourish.

That's frustrating. It does not serve people or propel them to where they really want to go.

I play drums. At a training event called "Fantasy Drum Camp," and also at a music clinic I attended recently, several world-class musicians all made the exact same remark, independently of each other:

"The thing I hate most about being on tour is _____."

How do you think they finished the sentence?

Do they hate being away from their families? Sleeping in hotel rooms? Eating at Taco John's? Battling the music industry mafia? Making some giant screw-up during a live performance?

I figured it would be something like "being trapped on a claustrophobic tour bus."

It wasn't any of those things. Here's what it was:

"The thing I hate most about being on tour is there's no time or place to practice. I love to practice."

If you want to be a super-successful marketer:

Put yourself in a position where you get paid to practice, even if it's only a modest amount of money. Practice until your "simple" karate punch—ad writing, making sales presentations, buying traffic, negotiating, whatever you love most—is endowed with incredible force. Learn to love repeating even basic things over and over again until you achieve perfection.

Don't fall in love with bright shiny objects. Fall in love with mastery.

What should you master? Some aspect of marketing or sales that you naturally love and excel at—harnessing the natural forces of who you are.

PARETO SUMMARY

▷ The most important thing in marketing is a unique selling proposition.

▷ Your business USP is an extension of your personal USP.

It's Not Failure.
It's Testing.

O K, so you've gotten *something* to work. You've gotten one or two sales. You've worked out a good USP. You've figured out how to find someone who's interested, say the right thing, and get a check. What do you do next?

1. Test, then
2. Scale up

Whenever you have something in your sales funnel that's not working, you just need to break it into pieces and make the first piece work. You don't look at it as failure; you think of it as an experiment that didn't work.

If you can't sell a product, see if you can give it away. Or give part of it away. If they won't take the free item, find out why.

Testing is hugely important. Testing is *scientific*. Twenty years ago, hardly anybody thought this way. Today if you don't think this way, you're fixin' to be roadkill.

You can test different sales stories, different headlines and offers just about anywhere: in person, on the phone, via email, print ads, or whatever. But if you want to make it clean-cut and as simple as possible, the best place to start is Google AdWords.

Why AdWords?

It would be natural for you to assume that the reason I say you should do this first is because I've created all kinds of books and courses about AdWords. Actually that's backward. The reason I wrote all those books and courses is because AdWords is the best place to start.

Why? Because AdWords is hands down the most advanced advertising machine in the history of humanity. Nothing else even comes close. Google gets 80 percent of the English language search engine traffic; Google is a source of very steady, reliable clicks.

AdWords lets you target any city, state, region, or country—you can target as narrow or wide as you want and in many markets—and it can send you tremendous quantities of traffic. You can set bid prices however you want and daily budgets; you can track everything with precision and measure ROI to the penny. You can stop your campaigns at will by pressing a pause button.

I also happen to think it's the fastest place for a person to learn and master the basics of results-accountable direct marketing. It's the gold standard.

AdWords works like this: If you sell voice mail systems, you open a Google AdWords account. You bid on keywords like:

> Voice mail
> Voice mail systems
> Voice mail software

You set a geographic territory (Houston, Texas / the whole state of Texas / the entire United States / US + UK + Canada + Australia) and a bid price. "I'm willing to bid $1.31 per click."

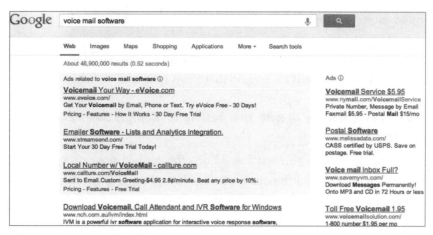

Figure 9–1. The shaded area at the top and the right side of a Google search are Pay-Per-Click AdWords ads.

Then your ads show up on Google when people search for "voicemail software" (see Figure 9–1).

In the screenshot in Figure 9–1, the three entries in the shaded area on the top and the listings running down the right side are all AdWords ads.

Google AdWords is an entire world unto itself, and if you're going to pursue it, I recommend my book *Ultimate Guide to Google AdWords*. (If you don't like my book, buy Howard Jacobson's or Brad Geddes' book. But whatever you do, don't even *think* about doing AdWords without getting educated first, cuz otherwise Google will vacuum out your wallet real fast.)

Also, stop what you're doing right now, and sign up for my free, online mini-course at www.perrymarshall.com/google. You can pull it up on your smartphone.

AdWords is a tester's dream machine. Let me show you the testing you can do with AdWords, simply by running multiple ads simultaneously.

The Unlimited Traffic Technique

I learned this from Jonathan Mizel, a reclusive mass consumer market-er who occasionally emerges from his cave in Maui, Hawaii, to teach a seminar or release a training course. He's a genius. Jonathan says that when you can convert a visitor to a dollar better than everyone else in your niche, you can buy *their* traffic from *them* because they'll make more money selling their visitors to you than they make by keeping the visitors to themselves.

This means that the most important thing you ever do is grow your Value Per Visitor. How do you do that? You split test.

How to Combine 80/20 with Split Testing to Multiply Sales 2X, 5X, 20X, and More

Split testing is when you test one ad or offer on half your prospects and another ad or offer on the other half. In the old days, split testing was an esoteric, direct-marketing concept that hardly anyone actually did. Now with Google and the internet, it's easy to do and quite necessary.

Here's a very common example of split testing two Google ads:

Popular Ethernet Terms	Popular Ethernet Terms
3 Page Guide—Free PDF Download	Complex Words—Simple Definitions
Complex Words—Simple Definitions	3 Page Guide—Free PDF Download
www.bb-elec.com	www.bb-elec.com
2 Clicks—CTR 0.1%	39 Clicks—CTR 3.6%

Notice what happened: All I did was reverse two lines—and the Click-Through Rate (CTR) jumped from 0.1 percent to 3.6 percent! (Click-Through Rate is the percentage of people who saw that ad and actually clicked on it.)

I've conducted entire seminars on all the quirky things you discover when you test Google ads. If you're buying Google ads and haven't gotten a thorough hands-on training, you're probably wasting all kinds of money on AdWords "stupidity tax."

For now, suffice it to say that changing even one word can have very significant effects on your results, easily plus or minus 50 percent. Just as you can test Google ads, you can split test landing pages, sales pages, product descriptions, photographs, and sales scripts.

Let's say your sales process looks like this:

1. Search engine ad or banner from consistent traffic source
2. Landing page offers a free report, software tool, video, free sample, or white paper in exchange for name, email address, etc.

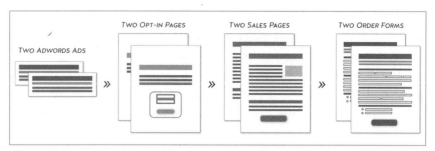

Figure 9–2. Serial Split Testing. (Illustration by Danielle Flanagan.)

3. Sales page (referred to in the report and by autoresponders)

4. Order entry page or telephone script

What we want to do is split test each of these four steps. We not only split test the AdWords ads, we split test two different landing pages, two different sales letters, and two different order forms. What happens if we do this? See Figure 9–2.

A *modest* goal would be to double the effectiveness of each step. This is not that hard to do. And you don't have to be a genius—you just need to try some sensible things.

So if we double the CTR of the AdWords ad, and the landing page, and the sales letter, and the order form, our improvement is

$$2 \times 2 \times 2 \times 2 = 16X.$$

A **16-times improvement** ain't nothing to sneeze at. **Notice that the improvements multiply, cascading from beginning to end. Every improvement is magnified in the end result!**

If you can triple each step, you get

$$3 \times 3 \times 3 \times 3 = 81X$$

You can make improvements early in the process faster and easier than late in the process, because you have more trials. A very realistic and likely set of improvements would be:

$$6 \times 3 \times 2 \times 1.5 = 54X$$

If you go into a competitive market on Google—like weight loss, travel, financial services, real estate, web hosting—it's very hard to win in these hyper-competitive categories. It's not unusual to start out losing money at a 4:1 ratio—that is, for every four dollars you give Google, you make only one dollar in gross profit.

But now you double each of these four steps—and you improve your numbers sixteenfold—now you're making $4 of profit for every $1 you give Google. That's pretty amazing. Continuous split testing is key to the whole thing.

Here's a very realistic scenario: six times improvement on AdWords, three times improvement in your opt-in page, a twofold improvement in your sales letter, and a 50 percent improvement in your order page (order pages are extremely sensitive to small changes—that sale hangs by a thin thread!), and now you've improved your conversion rate 54 times over what you started with.

To be honest, what you started with didn't have a chance! You probably made all kinds of assumptions that were wrong. We all do that. But split testing got you closer and closer to the right message until you hit pay dirt.

The promise of instantaneous traffic from Google is seductive and alluring. You've just finished your product, and you're eager to sell it. You may need the money. But many people are disappointed by their initial results, when in fact, once they've done testing, their chances of success are quite good.

When you're brand new at AdWords, you should look at your first few hundred dollars as a street MBA—the fastest and cheapest school of hard knocks and direct-marketing education you can get. It's not theory; it's live marketing combat. Only after you've acquired some experience should you expect it to be profitable.

By the way, don't feel bad if your very first salvo didn't stand a chance. *That's normal. That's 80/20.* Don't take it personally. Just try something else. In direct marketing, there is no failure. There are only tests that didn't work the way you thought they would.

PARETO SUMMARY

▷ Your first few hundred dollars of Pay-Per-Click advertising is pure education money. It's an affordable "street MBA," where you hone your marketing chops in the real world.

▷ If you want to fix a sales funnel, break it into pieces and fix the pieces.

▷ The secret to everything is split testing.

▷ Improvements in segments of sales funnels multiply.

Scale Up—Massively

O nce you've tested and done your homework—once you're scratching the right itches, once you're converting people at a healthy rate, you can massively expand your business.

Expanding into Other Media: Profiting from the Winner-Take-All Phenomenon

The winner-take-all phenomenon is the disproportionate advantage that any top dog has over all the others—that the top three players have over all the rest combined. It's like in the Olympics, where the gold medalist is world-famous and the silver and bronze medalists are busing tables two weeks later.

Winner-take-all is when 80/20 works in your favor. This is true on Google as well, and there's a snowball effect. You enter a market, you start split testing right away, and you use sound marketing techniques, copywriting, and all of the tools at your disposal.

How fast can you go from zero to dominating a market? *As fast as you can split test.*

80/20 for Ads

I've got a friend named Carlos Garcia. He's bought billions of clicks in his career. He's a maverick banner ad buyer, an invisible kingpin who steers huge volumes of web traffic. One time I asked him, "What's the secret of banner ads?"

"Test 50 ads. One of them's going to be a crazy winner."

You write 50 ads. Eventually, one of them's gonna fetch as much traffic as the other 49 put together. The good news is most people don't even test five. That's the 80/20 of ad writing, and in online advertising, testing is what separates the men from the boys.

Increase Your Sales 50 Times in 10 Steps

Pareto
Point

Let's say your chosen keywords get 100,000 searches per month on Google. Your ad shows every time someone does a search, and you start out with a 0.5 percent Click-Through Rate. That's your starting point. Here's what you do next:

1. Initially you're getting 17 clicks a day. You immediately test two ads against each other. Four days later, you've gotten 70 clicks, and you declare a new winner. You've doubled your CTR to 1 percent.

2. Now you're getting 33 clicks a day. After another three to five days you double your CTR again to 2 percent. Now you're getting 66 clicks a day, enough to declare a split test winner *every day*.

3. Your CTR inches up to 2.5 percent and to 3 percent. In two weeks you've already gone from 0.5 percent CTR to 3 percent CTR, a six-fold improvement—and your bid price remains the same.

4. Two weeks have gone by, and you've gotten a total of 400 visitors. Ten percent (40 of them) have opted in to your newsletter or downloaded your report, white paper, or whatever.

5. You start split testing different opt-in pages. You try a new headline or change some of your bullets.

6. You're getting 100 visitors a day. That's 70 new sales leads per week.

7. Within two to three weeks you can realistically double your opt-in rate from 10 percent to 20 percent. Now you're getting 140 leads per week. In time you may get that number up to 25 percent or 30 percent.

8. Now let's start counting the number of people who go from the sales page to the order form. You start out at 10 percent. That's 14 per week. Within a month you can test two to three new sales pages, and you have a realistic chance of doubling that 10 percent to 20 percent.

9. Testing conversion from the order form to actual orders is no different—28 per week. From what I've seen, a 10-percent conversion from order form page views to orders is reasonable. That's six orders per week, and within a month and a half we can probably improve your order form by 50 percent.

10. Another angle on the order form is to test **different price points, multiple offers, and upsells**. Multiple price levels and upsells can easily double or triple your profitability.

When you multiply all those numbers, your improvement from step 1 to step 9 is about fiftyfold. It took you two months to one year to do this. At this point, you're probably one of the best-performing players in your entire category.

Whether your product costs a hundred dollars or a million dollars, whether the last few steps are automated or manual, the principle is the same.

Ari Galper from Sydney, Australia, accomplished this in 10 months, growing his monthly sales from $5,000 per month to $100,000 per month.

Ari added an interesting twist: He worked the early ingredients in his sales funnel (like Google ads) with A-B split testing. But he improved his lead capture pages and sales pages by talking to customers on his website via live chat. Every time his chats indicated confusion on the page, he would change the page and alleviate the confusion.

Not only did Ari go from a fledgling business to a six-figure income, he transformed his Unlock The Game™ program into a respected international brand.

When you execute the 10 steps I described above, you get a world-class sales funnel. You dominate your market, and you easily expand *far* beyond AdWords.

Re-Inventing a Website from the Inside Out

Every website needs a makeover. Everybody's dissatisfied with their website. Most people spend months and months re-doing everything. You could spend the rest of your life chasing perfection.

Half the time, the improvements don't really make things better. Many of these projects cost tons of money and blatantly violate 80/20, because redoing a 500-page website takes months of labor and hardly anyone visits 80 percent of the pages.

Before you tackle the whole website, just pick the single most important page and split test variations. Improve, improve, improve, and you'll get half the total benefit and have to worry about only one page.

You can get almost all the improvement that is possible by optimizing a handful of key sales pages and perhaps your overall template. Whenever you find yourself obsessing over everything, you're making a mistake.

As for perfection: 80/20 inherently means that "good enough is good enough." When you embrace 80/20 there's always going to be some unfinished detail. Sometimes this will bother you.

The question is: Do you want perfection, or do you want success?

There will always be *something* in your success formula that demands perfection.

If you're a concert pianist, then every note must be right; 80 percent right will not do when you're performing at Lincoln Center in Manhattan. And in any company, profession, or success story, there is a very *small* number of things that truly have to be perfect.

Be encouraged to know that you can become successful and even famous by achieving perfection in one tiny corner of your world. And please remember that everything else just needs to be *good enough.*

You might be able to close 50 percent of the customers you present to, and your salespeople may be able to close only 25 percent. But if you want your company to grow, you'll need to accept their imperfection and move on to higher-value tasks.

The 21st-Century Path to Stardom

Have you heard of Tim Ferris' book *The Four-Hour Work Week*? The original title was *Drug Dealing for Fun and Profit*, a tongue-in-cheek name for what was essentially a book about outsourcing. His book publisher said, "No way, Jose, we're not using *that* title."

They bickered back and forth about titles. Finally Tim went to the court of last resort—real-world testing on real people. He posted book titles as Google ads, and the phrase "Four-Hour Work Week" magically spiked the response. He renamed his book and organized it around that concept. It became a *New York Times* bestseller.

Later came his bestsellers *The Four-Hour Body* and *The Four-Hour Chef,* and now he's the maestro of a hit series of books and much more.

By the way, I take my own medicine. The title of my AdWords book, *The Definitive Guide to Google AdWords,* was perfected with Google ads, as was the title of the book you're reading right now.

OK, So You Have a Killer Sales Process—Now What?

What you've done so far would have been *very* hard to do in the offline world. Before Google, it was not a whole lot easier in the online world, because there was never a consistent, controllable source of traffic.

Paid search engine traffic, like what you get from Google and Bing, is generally consistent. It's always 100 percent controllable. Within two to six months (not two to three years) you've tested several dozen ideas and eliminated all but the best. You've polished a sales process to the point where it delivers *killer* results.

You're making a killer ROI on your sales process. And because you're so effective at turning visitors into dollars, you can afford to pay more for your traffic than all your competitors. You're becoming unstoppable.

What now?

Now we go out with our growing war chest and buy all the traffic we can get, using my **expanding universe theory** of online marketing.

Applying the Expanding Universe Theory to Your Business

You've started out buying clicks literally one at a time and meticulously, patiently refined your marketing machine. So you take the same messages and sales process and roll out your product in this order:

1. Google AdWords
2. SEO
3. Other PPCs like Bing and display advertising
4. Email promotions
5. Social media*
6. Affiliates
7. Direct mail
8. Banner ads and ad networks
9. Press releases
10. Print advertising, TV, and radio

Items 2 through 10 are more expensive and/or less controllable than Google. Get it right with Google first, where you have total control, AND THEN do email. THEN get help from affiliates. Don't let any of these other things or people be your guinea pig—if it works on Google AdWords first, then you can invest in these other things and be fairly certain it will work.

Do you remember the famous self-help video *The Secret?* The creators used a very similar process to get their language and messaging—and their shopping carts and everything else—flowing like a well-oiled machine. They started by buying clicks and expanded from there. Then one day Oprah got excited about their product, and BAM! *The Secret* went viral, selling untold millions of copies.

Also I'd like you to notice where social media ranks on this list. Pay attention to the little asterisk (*) next to it. I don't put it at the top because it doesn't generate much sales for most companies. But where this fits on this list depends hugely on what kind of business you're in.

Since social media generally starts with Facebook, you can take a free test at www.IsFBforMe.com. It will tell you how Facebook-friendly your business is, with a score from 1 to 10.

If your score is 5, leave social media where it is in the Expanding Universe—right in the middle, item Number 5. If your score is 10, move it to priority number one. If your score is 1, move it to number 10. (And yes, if your Facebook score is 10, you should do Facebook before you do AdWords.)

The reason I created the IsFBforMe tool is sales is a disqualification process. I was applying the 5 Power Disqualifiers. When my Facebook advertising book came out, I knew I could convince a lot of people to try Facebook ads—but it would not work for them. I knew the only way to get happy customers and 5-star ratings on Amazon was to *dis*qualify people who didn't fit. I tell people: If you scored an 8 or above, Facebook ads will be very important for you. If you got less than a 6—you probably shouldn't even buy my book at all.

High scores on Facebook are businesses that sell **entertainment, tribal identity, experiences, and escapism.** Fiction books, music groups, movies, spirituality, local hangouts, aspirations, political causes, and travel generally perform well on Facebook.

Google Is the Yellow Pages. Facebook Is a Coffee Shop

Facebook is not where people go to buy, say, automotive brake pads. If you sell B2B, Facebook is probably almost useless, but LinkedIn may prove very useful. Ted Prodromou's book *Ultimate Guide to LinkedIn for Business* is an excellent reference.

In any case, how you expand from small to large in various media is hugely important. You do NOT just "sling mud against the wall." You start with the place of highest leverage and testing with consistent traffic, which is highly targeted paid advertising. You're actually starting at the top end of the Power Curve, testing the highest-quality traffic sources on a small number of people. Then you expand from there.

PARETO SUMMARY

▷ You can optimize most of your sales funnel by optimizing a handful of vitally important web pages. The rest can just be "good enough," at least for now.
▷ The expanding universe theory of market domination says you build out your advertising strategy in this order: paid search engine

traffic first, then email and affiliates, then social media, then offline media.

▷ How you prioritize social media varies hugely depending on the type of business you're in. Get your "Social Media Compatibility Score" at www.IsFBforMe.com.

Expand, Diversify, and Conquer Planet Earth

can't overemphasize how powerful the expanding universe principle is. Usually, search engine traffic represents **only a small percentage** of the people who are potential customers for you. When you roll out to items 2 through 10 (refer to page 82), you can often generate 5 to 50 times as much in sales as you were making with paid search engine traffic. And no longer is it necessary to risk more than a few thousand dollars on a marketing campaign!

By the way, you don't want to become exclusively reliant on AdWords (or Facebook or email or any other primary traffic source) over long periods of time. That's because Google can be temperamental and bid prices can easily fluctuate. You don't want too many eggs in any one basket. If you follow this strategy, you're automatically insulated from whatever minor disaster might turn up in one particular advertising channel.

I put print, TV, and radio last because they're generally the most expensive for direct-response marketing. However, if you do what I've shown you, you have the best chance of anyone of making them work. When you can make TV and radio work with an acceptable ROI, you can get huge volumes, with the bonus effect of brand awareness, mass exposure, and buzz.

The expanding universe principle goes on the 80/20 Power Curve too, as in Figure 11–1.

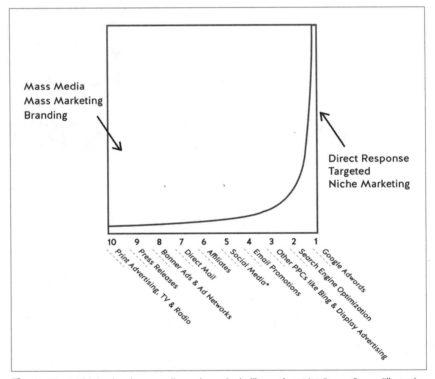

Figure 11–1. This is what the expanding universe looks like on the 80/20 Power Curve. (Illustration by Danielle Flanagan.)

Small, highly targeted audiences are on the right; large mass markets are on the left. The Y-axis measures *focus* and *efficiency*. You should always move from right to left, from narrow to wide, not the left to right.

"Branding" and mass exposure are on the *left* side of the Power Curve: high quantity, low quality. Laser-targeted traffic sources like search engine marketing and email lists (high quality, low quantity) are on the right. As you execute the expanding universe principle, you work your way down the Power Curve.

If you're a small company, you must concentrate your advertising dollars, kind of like when you were a kid burning leaves with a magnifying glass on a sunny day. You must hold your dollars accountable for results. Countless startups have gone to early graves because they tried to "get their name out there." They failed because they got egocentric and put branding and exposure ahead of building a solid, reliable sales funnel.

Resellers and Affiliates: The Momentum Kicks In

You never want your sales partners to be blind test subjects for your experiments. Friends come and go, but enemies accumulate.

Distributors, affiliates, resellers, channel partners, or whatever they're called in your particular industry, want to make money. They like to EAT. (Preferably today.) So the Holy Grail for an affiliate or distributor is a program that consistently sends him very good dollars in exchange for his customer's attention, as fast as possible.

Do your experiments with paid search engine traffic first. Then verify it with email promotions and inclusions in e-zines. Now that you have rock-solid numbers, take it to your affiliates.

Great affiliate relationships are *extremely* profitable. Brick-and-mortar sales channels and "feet on the street" likewise are a bankable asset. And more partners breed more partners. The snowball effect multiplies, and you get so much traffic you can't make it stop.

This is the solution to the yin and yang problem of specialization vs. diversity that I talked about earlier. When people naturally get paid well for sending you customers, you'll get customers from all kinds of diverse sources.

Treat Your Salespeople Like Valued Affiliates

You'll have much more success hiring and keeping good salespeople if the majority of your products have well-developed sales processes. A salesperson isn't all that different from a rep, distributor, or affiliate.

If you're still in the experimental stage with a product, then everyone deserves to know that. And if you've figured out a reliable way to sell your product, by all means, train your salespeople!

Kaizen: The Magnificent Power of Continuous Improvement

I worked in manufacturing for a long time, and the Japanese word *kaizen* is a household word in mass production, quality control, and management. *Kaizen* means "continuous improvement," and the real power of kaizen is the compound interest of that improvement over time.

If you've ever listened to investment and financial planning people, bankers, or lenders, you know the Rule of 72—it says that 72 divided by the interest rate tells you how fast the investment doubles in value. If you earn 12 percent annual interest, you double your money every six years, because $72/12 = 6$. Compound interest applies to marketing processes, too. The growth rates are much, much faster.

You've worked really hard for six months to get that 54-fold improvement in sales conversion, and now you're going to shift your focus. All you're going to do is split test a couple of things at each step of the process, one time per month. One more AdWords ad, one tweak to the opt-in page, one new version of the sales letter, and one version of the order form.

Half the time, the contender isn't an improvement at all. OK, so every month you get two new winners instead of four. The total improvement each month is still perhaps 5 percent for one and 5 percent for the other. The total improvement is 10 percent.

A 10-percent improvement each month means you double your throughput (customers passing through your funnel) every 7.2 months! You nearly quadruple your sales efficiency within a year. The 54X becomes 216X.

So when you add these other traffic sources—affiliates, banner ads (bargain priced if you do it right, and yes, they definitely work), and offline marketing sources, you get 10 times the traffic you were able to get from search alone, and the 216-fold becomes 2,160-fold.

That's right, two to three years later, your sales are a thousand times greater than they were the very first day you started. Admittedly, your first day was pretty dismal, but this should give hope to everyone who's launched a fledgling new venture.

"Is This Really Possible?"

It's not hype when I talk about 16X, 54X, 216X, and 2,000X improvements in sales and even greater gains in profitability. Here's why. First of all, understand that in highly competitive markets, where there are 30, 50, or even 100 advertisers bidding against you, AdWords is tricky and it definitely costs you money to do all that initial split testing. The barrier to entry can seem formidable. Most people give up too early.

But sales improvements happen in internet time, and that can be fast. Look at what happened to Google—they went from a certified nobody in

CRANE DISTRIBUTOR DOMINATES

Once I had a customer who sold industrial cranes. He replaced four salespeople with paid search engine traffic. He optimized everything to the hilt, just as I've described. He was doing very well, but to send his business through the stratosphere, he created new sites with different USPs, so he could attack the market from a new angle. He wasn't competing with himself, because the new sites appealed to completely different price motivations, service levels, etc. It's kind of like Pepsi owning KFC and Taco Bell.

He added both diversity and stability and was rapidly becoming a major player in the material handling industry. A year later, three of Google's 11 ad positions were occupied by his three companies, and he was gaining ground on the organic, free listings as well. He was also gaining exposure at trade shows and in industry magazines.

The last time I talked to him, a European conglomerate was inquiring about buying his mini-empire.

Take this information seriously. This is how you get wealthy with direct marketing. Once you start getting traction, it's onward and upward. The better your numbers at every step, the faster you get new results and the faster you make more improvements. You're able to buy more traffic and you become an internet juggernaut. An unstoppable force.

an already-crowded search engine market, to a billion dollars in sales in five years, to eclipsing all print media advertising in less than 15. By year 10 they were already one of the wealthiest companies in history.

The world is accelerating. The formula I just gave you is, in principle, the same formula Google used to become the killer search engine that it is—continuous *kaizen*—improvement based on true numbers, feedback, a "natural selection" marketplace process, and your own unique designs.

This is how you dominate your market. You can use the simple math I've provided, combined with the cost for clicks in your market, to figure out how much money you'll have to spend to become the top dog. In most cases it's not hundreds of thousands or millions of dollars—it's usually only a few thousand.

PARETO SUMMARY

▷ Unlimited traffic technique: When you have the best conversion rate in your niche, you can buy all the traffic from everybody.

▷ You should test your sales funnel yourself before you ask anyone else to sell it.

▷ Sometimes it's to your advantage to spin off other brands and add new USPs to the marketplace.

Make More From Every Customer
80/20 Economics

This is the most critical aspect of marketing, because you can have the best customer list in the world and best sales pitch in the world, but if your pricing strategy is lousy you'll still go broke. If your economics are bad, that means you're taping dollar bills to every product that gets shipped out the door. Better marketing only hastens your trip to bankruptcy court.

And please understand, the money *you* get is only half the equation. The other half of the equation is even more important: *How much **value** does the customer get?*

"Economics" is about **both** these things. It's central. Economics should always be the starting point of any marketing conversation. Especially if you're searching for a breakthrough and not just a minor improvement.

The first thing to understand about economics is it's 80/20 all the way up and down. If we line up 100 customers from least able to buy to most able to buy, AND least tempted by your proposition to most tempted, HERE, in Figure 12–1, is how they stack up:

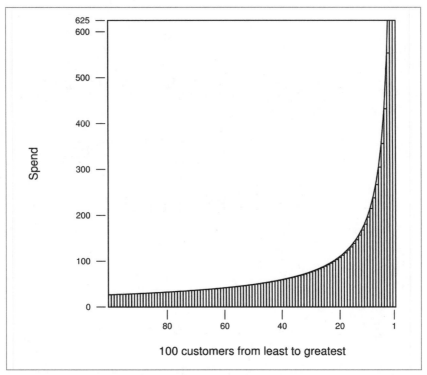

Figure 12–1. If 100 people give you an average of $100 each, the 80/20 Power Curve shows how much money each one wants to spend with you. The tool at www.8020curve.com allows you to plug in numbers and predict how many customers will spend different amounts of money.

A lot of people assume their customers are all roughly equal. They are not—not even close! That's the 80/20 Power Curve in action. This example assumes the average customer spends $100, and you collected a total of $10,000.

Here you see the least interested person wants to spend $27. The most interested person will spend $1,426 (notice he's way past the top of the chart). So the most interested person will spend 50 times more money than the least interested one.

It's also interesting to notice the people who actually spend the average amount, which is $100, are people near the "top 20 percent" mark. In other words—only 20 percent of these customers represent a serious opportunity for you.

Handy rule of thumb: 80/20 says that 20 percent of the people will spend 4 times the money. It also says that 4 percent of the people will spend 16 times the money. Memorize this—it's one of the most powerful facts you could ever know about business.

OK, So How Do You Use This Information?

The Power Curve shows you why McDonald's always sells small, medium, and large drinks. It's because peoples' capacity to consume varies widely. As you'll see in a minute, though, $1.00 for small, $1.40 for medium and $1.85 for large barely scratches the surface of peoples' true differences. But most important, the Power Curve shows you the almost limitless capacity of the top 1 percent. Which brings us to . . .

The Principle of the $2,700 Espresso Machine

Pareto Point

Let's say 1,000 people walk into a Starbucks shop today. The least anyone will spend is $1.40 for a "Tall" Coffee of the Day. Let's plug those numbers into the Power Curve and see what it tells us.

One thousand visitors means 1,000 members. The 1,000th member (the lowest-spending person in the lineup) spent $1.40. We enter the data like this at www.8020curve.com, in Figure 12–2 (page 94).

The graph it gives us is shown in Figure 12–3 on page 94.

When you click on "Examine a range of members," you can check up on Member Number One—your top-spending customer.

The tool predicts the customer *wants* to spend $537 at Starbucks today. How does a person spend $537 at Starbucks? Do they buy 100 lattes?

No. They buy three lattes, two blueberry scones, and one espresso machine! As I'm writing this, Starbucks' website features two espresso machines, shown in Figure 12–4, page 95.

Hey man—not only can you go home with a $275 espresso machine in hand, if you're feeling really ambitious, you can part with $2,699.95 and carry 45 pounds of stainless-steel coffee-making pleasure with you.

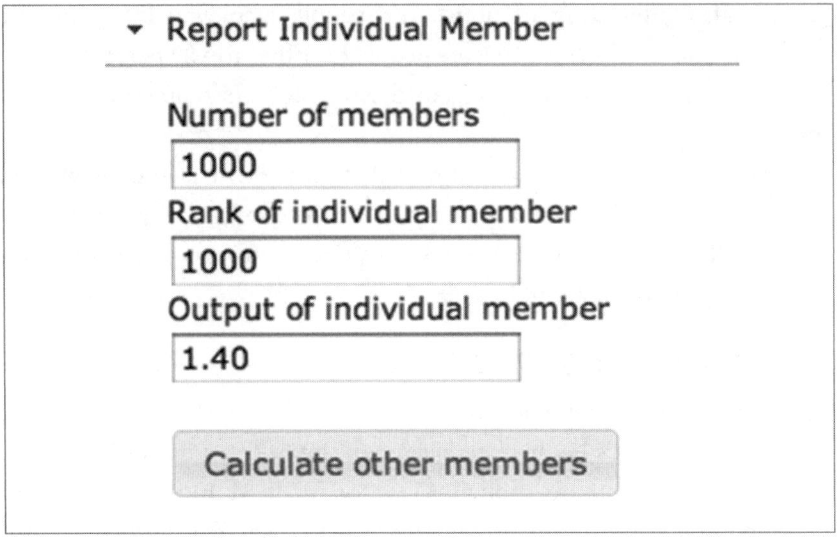

Report Individual Member
Number of members
1000
Rank of individual member
1000
Output of individual member
1.40
Calculate other members

Figure 12–2.

50
40
30
20
10
0
Spend
800
600
400
200
1
1000 Customers from Least to Greatest

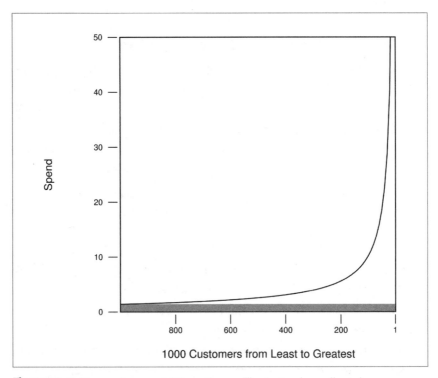

Figure 12–3. How much money 1,000 people are willing to spend on coffee today.

Musica Lux by Nuova Simonelli
$2,699.95

Aroma Espresso Machine by Saeco
$275.00

Figure 12–4. It's no accident that Starbucks sells a $200 espresso machine and a $2,000 espresso machine side by side.

Starbucks' 10X spread between the ordinary machine and the extraordinary machine is no accident, by the way. Them folks at Starbucks ain't dumb. They understand Power Laws. (Just think, if you give your mother-in-law the Musica Lux unit for Christmas, and she uses it 10 times, it only costs you $269 per cup of espresso.)

Joking aside, **the Espresso Machine Principle is a paramount strategy of successful business.** Yes, you can always find companies that ignore it. But most of them aren't doing well, and the Power Curve virtually *guarantees* you that they are leaving money on the table.

Hotels have $1,200-per-night suites on the top floor. Airlines have red carpet clubs for their top 20 percent customers. International flights offer $10,000 first-class seats and $20,000 luxury sleeping pods. For the airline, that sure is nice compared to getting $385 for a seat in coach.

The book *Whale Hunt in the Desert* by Deke Castleman describes how Vegas casinos get 20 percent of their income from a super-elite class of gamblers called "Whales." Whales fly in on private jets and bet $100,000 on a single round of blackjack. Casinos lavish Whales with dedicated staff, perks, amenities, and high-end luxuries that are utterly invisible to every other guest in the hotel.

80/20 doesn't just work in Vegas. A tiny $1-million charity will most likely get $100,000 of its donations from one single trust, foundation, or individual donor. A $200,000 per year one-man tax practice can and should get $20,000 of business from a single customer.

Mr. Smith's restaurant in Washington, DC, is "Home of the $1,000 Hamburger." Yes, they really do sell a hamburger for $1,000. (Their website insists it's really good.)

This is not merely about selling to the affluent, or conspicuous consumption, though you should never ignore either of those things. That's because the Espresso Machine Principle applies to **all** aspects of product and service sales:

- How much the unit costs.
- How often they come back and buy more. One espresso machine buyer in 50 will buy another one every week. (Probably not at Starbucks, but they'll buy it somewhere.)
- How many units they buy at one time. One espresso machine buyer in 50 is gonna want 100 units all at once.
- People who buy units in quantity, and often. One espresso machine buyer in 2,500 will want 100 units every week.

The Power Curve Is Multi-Dimensional

When you look at all your past buyers, the Power Curve applies to:

> **Repeat buys:** Of the people who buy more than once, 20 percent of them are responsible for 80 percent of the repeat purchases.
>
> **Money:** 80 percent of the overall money comes from 20 percent of the buyers.
>
> **Quantity:** How many units of a specific product bought at one time is on the Power Curve. 20 percent of the orders represent 80 percent of the quantity.
>
> **Diversity:** How many different types of products they buy at any one time is on the Power Curve. Twenty percent of the orders represent 80 percent of the diversity.

THE MAN WHO TRIPLED HIS BUSINESS IN FOUR MONTHS
WITH 80/20

Joshua Boswell, a freelance copywriter, came to a Four Man Intensive, one of my private workshops in February. I gave him an explanation of the Espresso Machine Principle and how it flows from 80/20.

Suddenly–he *saw* it. His brain lit on fire. He saw where a whole bunch of money was lying on the table. He understood exactly what he needed to do. And the first thing on the list was creating a new, high-end, "Espresso Machine" type offer for his client.

His client sold online training courses for currency traders. At the time, their most expensive product was a $500 set of manuals and DVDs that walked customers through a series of strategies for succeeding in that business. I showed him that if he could deliver the same thing in a more valuable way, he could pick up a large number of sales at a $2,000 to $3,000 price point.

The number-one thing his client was missing was *hands-on help.* Joshua transformed run-of-the-mill distance learning into hands-on mentoring. He organized a combination of one-on-one, look-over-shoulder guidance and small-group orientation sessions that tremendously increased the personal touch that students experienced.

In May he sent me this report:

Here are some basic dollar growth numbers for our business this year:

Month	Orders	Gross Revenue
January	396	$25,440.35
February	459	$29,365.90
March	684	$53,953.92
April	945	$76,847.40

Grand Total: 2,484 orders; $185,607.57.

Now, these following numbers are even more exciting to me. Look at the average amount our customers spend, per order:

continued

THE MAN WHO TRIPLED HIS BUSINESS IN FOUR MONTHS WITH 80/20, CONTINUED

January: $64.24

February: $63.97

March: $78.88

April: $81.32

Not only did our orders go up, but their average value increased as well. How cool is that? We added one quick upsell, and that made the difference.

Oh, and did I mention that we are only just starting?

What this means is that if all you sell is scones and cups of coffee ranging from $1 to $5, your business is probably doomed. And if it's not doomed, you're destined to earn a meager living and barely scrape by.

The principle of the $2,700 espresso machine applies to almost anything you might choose to sell. If your website just sells one book or one wedding candle or one exercise band for $29, you're leaving buckets of money on the table. Because if you just scratch one narrow itch on some super-specific topic, the intensity of that itch and the propensity to spend money to scratch it is easily 100:1. Selling that one book was merely a way to attract a long-term customer.

That means you can add a $290 product and a $2900 product, and you'll probably double your sales. If you have thousands of customers, the spread will be even wider. Many businesses do not have product offerings spanning a 100:1 range, so they're missing all kinds of opportunities to sell to their *existing* customers.

When you take full advantage of this, your sales and profits immediately go up, making it much easier for you to go get more customers. You can advertise more, bid more for clicks, promote yourself in more media channels, pay more for leads.

Deliver Value

Obviously, you can't sell the same cup of coffee for $1 to some people and $10 to others in the same place at the same time. (Not usually anyway.) But the point of the Power Curve is if coffee is the itch, the range of expense they'll go to scratch it is huge. The initial $1 cup of coffee is a rack-the-shotgun exercise.

The 80/20 principle says that if 10 people will pay $1 for a cup of coffee, two of the 10 will pay $4 for a better cup of coffee. As long as the superior cup of coffee is perceived as being "just as good of a deal" as the ordinary one, you can be reasonably certain that those two will step up to the plate and spend the extra money.

The core question people ask when they pay money is: "What problem can you solve that nobody else can solve?"

Starbucks famously addressed this question by utterly transforming the coffee experience. The concept of a gourmet coffee in a luxury environment with exquisitely appointed decorations and aromas—cappuccinos and lattes and jazz—all that was very strange when Starbucks set out to make their cup of coffee "the $3 luxury that almost everyone can afford." That's their USP.

Many have forgotten that in the 1980s, coffee was an uninspiring brown beverage that cost 65 cents, served in a Styrofoam™ cup with a packet of sugar with some chalky powder that people insultingly called "creamer."

Any business can be transformed the way Starbucks transformed coffee. It doesn't matter if it's insurance, or metal stampings, or jet airplanes; a "gourmet" version is always possible. This can transform the entire industry. Starbucks completely changed the very idea of coffee and inspired thousands of imitators.

PARETO SUMMARY

> ▷ At any given price point, 20 percent of the people will spend four times the money.
> ▷ The Power Curve (www.8020curve.com) shows you the "propensity to buy" in your customer base, even if you have data on only one single product.

▷ The Espresso Machine Principle says that a business based on many small transactions can make just as much money from a few large transactions.

▷ Most businesses are leaving all kinds of money on the table, and the Power Curve shows you where it is.

13

Power Guarantees

Three years after I got out of college, I was laid off from my job as an engineer. My wife was three months pregnant and planned to quit her job as a legal secretary when she had our new baby. The pressure was on.

I scrambled around looking for jobs. I couldn't find any engineering jobs that were a good fit so I went into sales. I met a great guy named Wally who said, "I think Perry is a sales guy waiting to happen." I took a job at his rep firm, selling industrial components.

Every day I went into the office and started making phone calls. Sales was much harder than I had imagined. For a year and a half I struggled mightily to get traction, living on skinny commission checks, eating baloney sandwiches and ramen soup, roiling in frustration.

A Wisconsin manufacturer we represented assembled custom circuit boards. At that time, "surface mount" technology was fairly new, replacing old-fashioned "through-hole" components. I needed to find customers who wanted to switch from old to new.

After months of calling, I finally found a customer who was right on the cusp and had an immediate need—a bleeding neck. One afternoon, Wally called and was very excited. This customer was asking to meet with our manufacturer in Milwaukee and was seriously considering converting their entire product line from through-hole to surface mount.

This would generate a significant amount of business for at least two years, generating nearly half a million dollars. If we did a good job, we might keep their business for years. I did the math in my head and instantly knew: This would finally be the thing to move me and Laura from the red to the black.

It would also move me from being a liability for Wally to being an asset.

Wally and I drove up to Milwaukee, excited. On our way, Wally expressed concern about the recent sale of one of the manufacturer's divisions.

We got there and met with our customer's head of engineering and director of purchasing. We took a tour of the Milwaukee factory. Mightily impressed, the engineering manager said, "Let's look at the engineering department where you guys will be redesigning these boards for us."

John, the sales director for the manufacturer, suddenly becomes deferential and says, "It's on the other side of that door, and that division just got sold to another company yesterday. We have a freelancer who's going to be doing the conversion. That freelancer is Steve. Here, meet Steve."

The engineering manager got aggressive and began firing questions at Steve. Steve started stammering, withering under the man's gaze and struggling to respond to his demands with confidence. The manager simply did not believe their pleas to trust them and believe that they were really up to the task.

That meeting went downhill fast. The engineering manager and his director of purchasing left in a huff and ever after refused to return my phone calls.

Over a span of almost two years, a half-dozen major projects failed in very similar ways. Over and over again, the companies I represented were unable to guarantee the level of customization or performance that my customers demanded.

It was only much later that I fully understood my core problem: My manufacturers wanted to sell only off-the-shelf, commodity items. They sold components, but they didn't offer complete solutions and they didn't guarantee results. I learned the hard way: **There's nothing worse than selling for a company that won't stand behind what you promise.**

Later, I would also discover: There's nothing better than selling for the only company who will stand behind you.

The Incredible Magnetism of a Power Guarantee

The pharmaceutical industry is about as conservative as conservative gets. It resists change. Why? Because if contaminated medicine is injected into a patient's veins and the person dies, the pharmaceutical company gets hit with a multimillion-dollar lawsuit, regulatory fines, and potential closure of the business.

The pharmaceutical guys don't change *anything* just for the fun of it. Ever. Especially their manufacturing equipment. So when my friend and colleague Tom Hoobyar founded a startup in Silicon Valley that made pharmaceutical tank valves, he had to *completely eliminate* the risk of anything going wrong for his customer.

So he made an enormously ballsy guarantee. See Tom's guarantee on page 104.

Tom's valves cost $4,000. If anyone invoked his guarantee and demanded that ASEPCO replace the customer's valve with a competitive unit, the total cost of parts and labor added up to about $40,000.

That'll sink your ship real fast if you're not on top of your game. So Tom's guarantee forced everything that happened *before* the customer got his product to be right. It placed demands on purchasing, receiving, inventory, quality control, shipping, and sales. Everything from beginning to end had to be a tight ship.

ASEPCO's Unique Tank Valve Guarantees
Lifetime Free Replacement of
Any Broken ASEPCO Tank Valve—No Matter Who Broke It!
Top-Quality Product, Or It's Free!
On-Time Delivery, Or It's Free!
Performance As Promised, Or We Pay You!

We do more than **make** promises. We live up to them. All ASEPCO employees are company shareholders, so we agonize over the quality of everything we ship. The only way we can prosper is by helping you succeed.

Top-Quality Product or It's Free!

If your ASEPCO valve contains a manufacturing defect, we will FIX OR REPLACE YOUR VALVE—AND WE WILL NOT BILL YOU!

On-Time Delivery or It's Free!

If you give us written notice at the time of your order that a valve delivery is time-critical and we make a written commitment to that date, IF WE ARE EVEN ONE MINUTE LATE YOUR VALVE WILL BE FREE!

Performance as Promised or We Pay You!

If it is proven that a properly assembled ASEPCO valve is not CIP/SIP in use,

   a) We will buy back our valve for a full refund.

   b) We will buy you the replacement valve of your choice.

   c) AND we will pay the documented cost of replacing it in your ASME tank!

Lifetime Free Replacement of Any Asepco Tank Valve, No Matter Who Breaks It!

Sometimes a tank is dropped—sometimes a valve gets hit by a forklift. No matter how a valve is broken or who's at fault, we will replace it free! No arguments. No excuses. Just a free replacement valve as fast as we can make it.

You can depend on ASEPCO products. And you can depend on us.

Tom had an average of about four of these claims per year, so he had to budget $160,000 into his annual marketing budget for guarantee payouts. This was a marketing expense. And, of course, every time there was a claim, he had to examine his entire company from stem to stern and fix whatever process was broken.

This is how ASEPCO achieved 90 percent market share in 15 years in one of the world's most conservative industries, going toe-to-toe with solidly established $100-million companies.

Most B2B marketers are terrified of making Power Guarantees. Power Guarantees are rare as hen's teeth. Why? Because making a guarantee this bold terrifies everyone in the company.

If it doesn't make your stomach churn, it's probably not an awesome guarantee. Think about it for a minute: When a customer buys ASEPCO's valve, *somebody* is taking a risk. When somebody buys a $50,000 software package, *someone* is taking the risk. When somebody buys a $200,000 printing press, *somebody* is taking the risk.

The question is: Who is taking the risk?

And . . .

If YOU won't take the risk, why should your customer?

Your ability to take this risk has everything to do with *disqualifying* customers who do not fit. Remember the Five Power Disqualifiers? If you're going to make a guarantee, some of the disqualifiers are:

- Is the customer willing to follow all the steps necessary to use or install your product?
- Do they obey instructions? Do they cooperate with you and your staff?
- Do you have a definite process for determining whether they did the right steps or not?
- Are all the right steps laid out? Is it simple and clear and black and white?
- Do you have a way of determining whether the customer really is a fit *before* any money changes hands?

That's **disqualification**. In the Five Power Disqualifiers, it's a not-so-obvious aspect of "Do they have the ability to say yes." A company willing to write a check but not do their part to install or implement your solution and then blame you for it isn't saying yes.

This actually makes it *easier* for you to sell, because this is what you're saying to the customer:

"IF you pay us $4,000 and IF you install our [widget] correctly and IF you follow all the steps and IF your system is up to spec, THEN I guarantee you that our [widget] will be [sterile and operate perfectly and yada yada] OR ELSE I'll pay to have the [widget] ripped out and install the competitor's [widget] instead.

"Oh, and nobody else makes a guarantee like that. If you qualify and obey the instructions, *I guarantee you this will work.*"

That's a Power USP.

Master Formula for a Power USP

Pareto Point

If you are _____ (qualifying type of customer or company) and if you _____ (commit X dollars and follow steps Y and Z), then you will achieve _____ (specific results) or else _____ (penalty to me, your vendor).

That Power USP gives you the ability to charge more than everybody else, because *you deliver results.* Hour for hour, dollar for dollar, even though your product costs more initially, in the end it costs less. Less uncertainty. Less doubt. Less finger-pointing. Less going 'round in circles.

This is far more meaningful than the usual "satisfaction or your money back" guarantee that is so common in business-to-consumer marketing, most people have become blind to it. It's pretty unusual in B2B. But when you do it, you should phrase it such that nobody can ignore it.

This forces the customer to demonstrate his worthiness to be your customer in the first place. It makes them chase you instead of you chasing them. It's *takeaway selling.*

This also brings you better, smarter customers. Customers who want only the cheapest possible solution right this minute are usually terrible customers. Customers who understand the value of getting the job done right the first time are much more pleasant to work with. You get the best of both worlds: more money *and* better people.

One of my favorite sayings, which I stole from the venerable copywriter Herschell Gordon Lewis, is: Sell results, not procedures.

Any time you want to figure out how to get more money for what you sell, ask yourself this question:

"How do I make what I give my customer more of a finished result and less of a procedure?"

People Pay for Certainty

When I was 32, with three young kids, a car payment, and a mortgage, I parachuted out of my Dilbert Cube job and started a consulting firm, my current company. When I left, I didn't have any clients lined up, so I had to scramble to cover the bills.

A company I'd dealt with at my old job called me and wanted me to come to Arkansas and discuss a possible consulting gig. My wife Laura took one look at me and said, "Perry, you have to look the part. Time for you to own a good suit." She took me to Woodfield Mall near Chicago to buy one.

We arrived at the mall on a Sunday afternoon, and we went to J.C. Penney. We spent about five minutes looking around, during which time nobody even appeared to be working the floor. Suddenly she grabbed me by the arm and made a beeline for Nordstrom.

I gulped. "Nordstrom? That's where *rich* people shop." Dang. I grew up in Nebraska, for crying out loud. I never imagined buying anything at Nordstrom, ever.

Laura walks up to the guy in the men's department, a very distinguished-looking gentleman in his late 50s, and says, "My husband is starting a consulting assignment on Tuesday, and he needs a suit."

He calmly and deftly begins asking questions, laying garments over his arm and making recommendations. Within a few minutes I'm trying on a pair of slacks and a mock turtleneck and a sport jacket. Shortly after that he's measuring me and agreeing to have all my new clothes tailored and ready for pickup by 3 p.m. Monday.

$1,200 later, I'm the owner of a brand-new business casual outfit, sharp and perfectly fitting for a young, up-and-coming consultant.

Twelve hundred dollars? For clothes??? Doesn't my wife know I'm a geek? How did this happen?

Because I knew, and Laura knew, that because we'd gone to Nordstrom, *I looked right.* When I arrived in Arkansas bidding on my very first gig, I *knew* I looked right.

Keep in mind, I'm one of those guys whose wife picks out his clothes for him, because my own judgment of "what looks right" is shaky at best.

By the way, I got the consulting gig: $15,000 for two months of work, which was a very respectable start.

What's the difference between a $500 outfit from J.C. Penney and a $1,200 outfit at Nordstrom?

Confidence.

How much is that worth?

I came home with agreement in hand, working from my basement office. *I escaped the Dilbert Cube. I got my first paying gig. My bills are paid, and I'm on my way up. And I'm not going back.*

PARETO SUMMARY

▷ The essence of getting more money for what you sell is: "Sell results, not procedures."

▷ If you want to command higher prices than anyone else, then guarantee better results than anyone else.

▷ If you're selling for a company that lacks the will or ability to guarantee results, get yourself a different job.

▷ Master formula for a Power USP: "If you are _____ (qualifying type of customer or company) and if you _____ (commit X dollars and follow steps Y and Z), then you will achieve _____ (specific results) or else _____ (penalty to me, your vendor)."

▷ A Power USP makes every high-end sale a *takeaway* sale, which means customers are chasing you—you're not chasing them.

14

80/20 = Harnessing Natural Forces

Ken McCarthy, the mentor who recommended Richard Koch's *The 80/20 Principle*, is a pioneer in internet education. He organized the first internet marketing seminar in 1995 with Netscape founder Marc Andreessen.

"Good marketing always harnesses natural forces," Ken says. "When something works in the marketplace, there's almost certainly a prevailing wind or force that you're cooperating with, that makes it possible. It's a huge mistake to fight nature."

The genius of 80/20 is, it harnesses hidden forces in nature that are far more powerful than you would have suspected.

How and why does 80/20 work?

It works because of *chaos* and *feedback*. I believe it's very important for you to gain a wider picture of 80/20. We're going to leave the business world for a few pages. Then, armed with some new insights, we'll return to the business theme with even more tools in your tool belt.

Where the Exponential Power of 80/20 Comes From

I'll never forget my first trip to the Grand Canyon. It's just so *huge*. It's hard to believe that all it takes to create something like that is weather, water, and time. (See Figure 14–1.)

Figure 14–1. Canyons are structures where water has worn channels in the stone over thousands of years. The wearing of water is positive feedback, and the depth of the channels obeys 80/20. (Photo by Flickr/MoyanBrenn ©2011, used under Creative Commons license.)

The Grand Canyon perfectly illustrates 80/20 because once upon a time, a flat slab of rock came to the surface of the land and the water began to wear it away. With every receding tide, water drained away, taking the path of least resistance, wearing that channel ever so slightly deeper. A slight indentation became a groove, which became a crack, which became a crevasse.

With every rainfall, it became that much easier for water to take that path, until the water had no choice *but* to take that path. A very slight inclination once upon a time grew into an irreversible destiny through the power of erosion.

The erosion that creates rivers and streams and the Grand Canyon is **positive feedback.** Positive feedback is when past action reinforces future action, in the same direction. This is the exact opposite of **negative feedback,** which corrects errors. Cruise control keeps your car clicking down the highway at a steady 70 miles per hour, but if your car goes over 70, a negative signal reduces the pressure on the accelerator; it corrects it to 70 miles per hour. Negative feedback steers a guided missile or keeps a Segway electric vehicle perfectly balanced.

Positive feedback is the feedback of reinforcement instead of the feedback of correction.

Positive feedback is the root cause of chaos.

Figure 14–2. The regular but inexact pattern of these sand dunes is created by chaos–the same force that drives 80/20. (Photo by Flickr/mikebaird ©2008 Mike Baird, used under Creative Commons license.)

The sun shines on a black rock. The rock heats up, warming the air around it. The air around it expands, and because the air density goes down, it rises. This makes room for the air below it to flow past the rock and also become warm. Air flows around the rock and affects the air patterns nearby. It generates wind.

When you string together hundreds or millions of these tiny systems, you get . . . *weather*. The repetitious, ever-familiar, but never perfectly predictable nature of clouds and weather is a grand phenomenon that scientists formally study as chaos.

Chaos Theory isn't about disorder and disaster as its name might suggest. It's the patterns and regularity of complex systems. Chaos is where fractals come from. It's why all snowflakes have the same six-sided shape but every one is different. The same math that describes chaos also describes 80/20. If you're curious about this, check out the Appendix.

Just as water transforms a slight indentation into the Grand Canyon, 80/20 amplifies your own power. I used to listen to motivational tapes all the time, believing that I could transform the world with action and willpower. Mostly I only managed to make myself weary and didn't accomplish much. It was because I was not harnessing natural forces; I was actually working against them.

In business, when you harness natural forces, everything you do becomes easier and more effective. Why sculpt sand dunes with your back and shovel when the wind is perfectly willing to do most of the work for you?

That's what happens when you flow *with* 80/20 instead of resisting it.

The Amazing Power of Feedback

A 14-year-old boy takes his first drink of Jack Daniels and likes it. Thirty years and 10,000 drinks later, he's an alcoholic. *Positive feedback*.

An 11-year-old girl gets a standing ovation at her piano recital. She drinks in the applause, and 25 years later she appears in a black evening gown at Lincoln Center in Manhattan, where she plays Beethoven's Symphony #2 with the New York Philharmonic. *Positive feedback*.

Why is there always a second 80/20, and a third, and a fourth?

The same reason why on that rock, water wears away a groove within a groove within a groove.

The cycles of positive feedback loops create **self-similarity.** The large pattern looks exactly like the small pattern. Water seeping into a mud puddle in your front yard on a rainy day, in Figure 14–3, left, looks almost exactly the same as the as the edge of a lake seen from an airplane, in the right side of Figure 14–3.

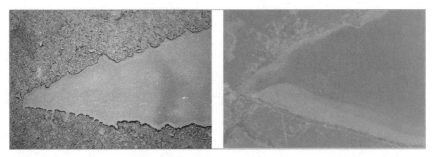

Figure 14–3. This tiny puddle of water on concrete (left) looks very similar to the edge of this lake in northern Michigan (right), even though the lake is tens of thousands of times bigger. Macro imitates Micro. (Photo credits: left, Shutterstock; right, United States Geologic Survey.)

This means that when you zoom in or zoom out 10X, 100X, and 1,000X, you see the same pattern over and over.

Positive Feedback Is Phenomenally Powerful

Ever turned up a PA system too loud, or let a microphone wander too close to a speaker? The system squeals and howls. That's positive feedback—the output is going right back to the input, and the energy grows exponentially.

If you inch the volume level carefully, the system begins to ring just a little bit. Inch it up more, and it slowly begins to howl. Inch it up a little more, and it deafens everyone in the room.

The sensitivity of that threshold shows you the incredible power of positive feedback. That range between no feedback and howling is pretty narrow. It's a *leverage point* in the system, a place where a tiny amount of effort generates a big result.

You get good at 80/20 by learning to identify the leverage points. In fact, it takes only a little bit of information to figure out exactly what those leverage points look like. Coming up: a software tool that makes it easy.

PARETO SUMMARY

▷ Any time you have positive feedback, you get 80/20 behavior.

▷ 80/20 is about harnessing natural forces. The same laws that make rivers, canyons, and sand dunes will also help you sell more and make more, if you let them. Wherever possible, let nature amplify your efforts by leveraging positive feedback and the patterns it creates.

▷ Rewarding people over time is just as powerful as water flowing on rock.

15

Do You Wanna Make $10 Per Hour? Or $100, $1,000, or $10,000?

D o you want to give your self a raise? Apply the 80/20 Power Curve to the time you spend in your day.

An 8-hour day has 480 minutes. Let's say you get paid $20 per hour. How much is the work you do actually worth? $20/hour x 8 hours/day = $160. If we look at your day in terms of 8 hours, it looks like this:

Number of members = 8

Total output of members = $160

The Power Curve, in Figure 15–1, page 116, shows that the least valuable hour in your $160 day is worth $8.96 and your most valuable hour is worth $53.74.

It gets even more interesting if we divide your day into 480 minutes:

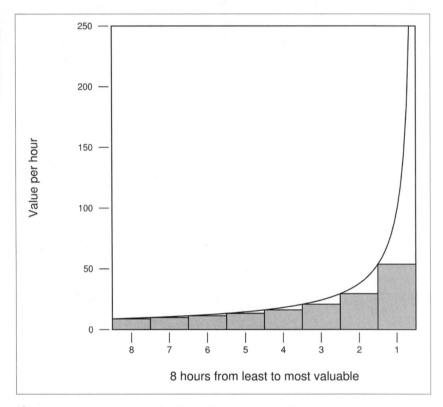

Figure 15–1. Actual value of eight different hours in your day, if you earn $20 per hour.

- Your average earnings per minute is 33 cents.
- The least valuable minute of your day is worth 7.6 cents.
- The most valuable minute of your day is worth $15.49.

Fifteen bucks a minute? Now what does this actually mean?

It means that when you're filing your fingernails or chatting with your friends on Facebook, your value to your employer is very low. To say you're worth 7.6 cents per minute to your employer while you're texting your fishing buddy is generous, to say the least.

It also means most people really get only about one to two hours of real work done each day and the rest of it is busy-ness. It means the true 80/20 individual can work one day a week and take the other four off. You just have to make that day really COUNT.

What activity is worth $15 per minute for an entry-level employee?

Answering the phone professionally and competently; finding an error in an invoice; paying close attention in a conversation and relaying critical information to another staff member. Greeting visitors in such a way that creates an overwhelmingly positive impression; paying someone a sincere compliment and brightening the atmosphere of the office; noticing that a customer has a problem that is easily solved, and solving it without delay.

You see here that the most valuable 30 minutes of a $20-per-hour employee's time is actually worth $150 per hour. Also notice: 15 dollars per minute is $900 per hour. Did you notice that?

For at least one minute a day, even a $20/hour employee is worth nearly a thousand bucks an hour. Which means a $200-per-hour employee (doctor, lawyer, business owner) is worth ten thousand dollars an hour. Wow!

"Can I Get a Raise? A Thousand Bucks an Hour, *Por Favor.*"

You increase your income by focusing on all these activities and find some other way, or some lower-paid person, to do the low-value activities. *You move resources from the left side of the curve to the right side.*

When you do that, you are suddenly on a new curve . . . but the curve is still the same shape. You're on a $50-per-hour curve instead of a $20-per-hour curve And guess what?

- The least valuable minute in your day is worth 19 cents.
- The most valuable minute in your day is worth 39 dollars.

So you're always climbing, climbing the Power Curve. In doing so, you naturally create opportunities for people below you, and they start climbing the curve, too.

The Power Curve permanently alters how you think about time.

About a year after I started my consulting firm, my friend Michael Cage mentioned that he was starting to make a lot of money doing teleseminars: Getting 10 or 100 or even 1,000 people on a conference call, and selling something.

I enlisted the help of my friend John Paul Mendocha and carefully scripted a presentation about replacing cold calling with guerilla marketing.

I invited my subscribers to listen in, I got 200 people on the line, and in one hour I sold $11,000 of products and consulting. Ten thousand bucks an hour. Wow. *Dang. I sold as much money in that one hour as I usually sell all month.* Once you have an experience like that, you'll never forget it, and you'll never want to go back to the old way.

That was about two weeks after I'd read Richard Koch's 80/20 book. I realize that I'd inadvertently applied 80/20, and I needed to master the 80/20 principle. A hundred thousand dollars per year equals 2,000 hours at $50 per hour. Most people think of those hours as roughly equal, but nothing could be further from the truth.

The typical $100,000-per-year person spends the vast majority of their time doing trivial $10-per-hour tasks, a decent amount of time doing $100-per-hour jobs, and occasionally—and somewhat accidentally—executing highly productive, $1,000-per-hour tasks. You can verify this for yourself; all you have to do is watch people closely. Even highly paid executives waste large spans of time on low-value activities.

In the last chapter I showed how even a $20-per-hour, $40K-per-year person probably spends at least one minute each day earning $900 per hour; he or she just doesn't know it. And once you're aware of this, you see the huge disparity. It doesn't take a genius to realize there's even more $1-per-hour tasks, plus a very few $10,000-per-hour tasks.

For a secretary, $10,000-per-hour opportunities do exist, but they aren't exactly plentiful. But you're in sales and marketing. Maybe you even own the company.

If you strongly influence sales in your company, $10,000-per-hour opportunities are everywhere around you. Which means if you're making less than $100,000-per-year, you won't be for long if you follow the 80/20 principle.

Let's rank your opportunities in dollars per hour (see Figure 15–2).

Notice that many times $10,000-per-hour jobs don't pay off until a lot of $10- and $100-per-hour infrastructure has been put in place. Tragically, so many million-dollar ideas don't see the light of day because one person

Pareto
Point

$10 per hour	$100 per hour	$1,000 per hour	$10,000 per hour
Running errands	Solving a problem for a prospective or existing customer	Planning and prioritizing your day	Improving your USP
Talking to unqualified prospects	Talking to a qualified prospect	Negotiating with a qualified prospect	Creating new and better offers
Cold-calling (of any variety)	Writing an email to prospects or customers	Building your sales funnel	Repositioning your message and position
Building and fixing stuff on your website	Creating marketing tests and experiments	Judging marketing tests and experiments	Executing "bolt from the blue" brilliant ideas
Doing expense reports	Managing Pay-Per-Click campaigns	Creating Pay-Per-Click campaigns	Negotiating major deals
Working "social media" the way most people do it	Doing social media well (this is rare)	Doing social media with extreme competence (this is very rare)	Selling to high-value customers and groups
Cleaning, sorting	Outsourcing simple tasks	Delegating complex tasks	Selecting team members
Attending meetings	Customer follow up	Writing sales copy	Public speaking
Driving to meetings			Establishing values and culture
Making trips to the store			
Performing basic customer service			
Building websites			
Spelling everything perfectly			

Figure 15–2. Some jobs are worth 1,000 times more than others. How are you spending your time?

is so bogged down in $10- and $100-per-hour jobs that they just never finish.

Plus, the person capable of recognizing and executing $10,000-per-hour tasks is usually bored stiff by $10-per-hour work. The fastest way to find more $1,000-per-hour opportunities is to simply get somebody else to do your $10-per-hour jobs.

I know what you're saying: "But my company will never hire an assistant for me." That's right, they won't. Hire him or her out of your own pocket.

The average, non-80/20 sales rep will never do this. (In fact, a surprising number of sales reps won't even buy a book about sales and learn how to improve themselves.) Every solo entrepreneur is sorely tempted to do everything himself. But let me explain why the smart ones swim against the stream and outsource anyway.

Outsource the Easy Stuff First!

Most of the items in the $10 column are pretty easy to hand off to someone else—bills, receipts, checking voicemail, etc. But if you're just starting out, you should also seriously consider getting someone else to do household tasks like:

- Washing clothes
- Cooking
- Cleaning
- Shopping
- Putting gas in the car

This will easily free up 10 hours per week. In most cities, other people will do stuff like this for $10 per hour. Your productivity doesn't have to improve that much to pay for the help you're hiring—and remember, you don't have to pay them until two weeks after they start!

Business tasks are tricky to outsource. A lot of people try to outsource things like copywriting and Google campaigns (hard to hand off successfully) when they should really be hiring a kid to mow their lawn or shovel the snow.

Sometimes the handiest person available for stuff like this is your spouse. That's where Laura and I were 15 years ago—a 20-something couple taking care of a little baby and spinning a thousand plates.

IS YOUR CASH *REALLY* TIGHT? DO THIS

If you barely have any money to spare, you can buy four hours of help per week for twenty bucks. You can hire virtual assistants online, often overseas for $5 per hour or less. Sometimes you can even find domestic or local help for that little money.

You will probably have to sift through a few to find a good one—and you should *expect* to. But they can speed all kinds of tasks for you. "Suzie, can you please research this for me, and get back to me tomorrow?" Handing off simple requests like that easily frees up several hours per week. Most important, it reduces your stress.

Now, begin every day with a question:

"What items on my to-do list can I hand off to my personal assistant?"

You will find that you can usually give one-fourth to one-half of your list to your assistant. The feeling you get when you can cross 10 things off your list *and not have to do any of them yourself* is wonderfully addictive.

The nice thing is, you don't have to fill all that extra time with work. You can enjoy your family and do fun things, too. (Imagine that!) If you have a traditional job this is *still* a great strategy—but you must be respectful of any issues your employer may have with this.

As soon as you have *any* margin, as soon as you're starting to get *any* traction at all, you need to start handing off those $10-per-hour tasks to others. When is it OK to do this? As soon as you're personally earning $100 per hour on any kind of consistent basis.

Take Back Your Life!

The point of making $100 or $500 or $1,000 per hour is not to become a slave to your work but to be the *master* of it. This book isn't just about selling more. It's about getting your life back! It's about regaining a sense of control, of setting your own priorities. It's about being able to take that three-week vacation and shut off your cell phone—without guilt.

Not long ago, a guy came up to me at a seminar and told me that his mother had gotten sick and he'd spent the last two years by her side. He had learned his marketing chops in Planet Perry, he'd mastered 80/20, and when the bad news came that she had a terminal illness, he knew exactly what to do.

He shifted gears and did what was really important to him. There he was thanking me for what he'd learned. We enjoyed a hearty handshake.

Most people experience some degree of heartburn about hiring "servants." It feels elitist. It seems very strange to have someone coming over to your house, doing stuff that your mother used to pay your allowance for. It may go against everything you were ever taught.

Get over it.

1. The **only** way you may ever achieve the real, interesting, fascinating, über-productive things that you really *want* to accomplish in your life—your Big Contributions and your "bucket list"—is by shedding a whole bunch of utterly forgettable, trivial, uninteresting busy work.

2. Somebody **wants** that job. As a matter of fact, they were praying that a job would come along, just yesterday. YOU are the answer to their request. Your "inner head trash" about achieving great things and exercising your authority only robs them of their opportunity to climb the ladder.

3. This is the fastest, easiest way to solve the unemployment problem. If 5 percent of the people in the world hired a personal assistant, 10 percent unemployment would suddenly become 5 percent. And you already know that the top 5 percent of people in the world can well afford the extra help.

You were not put on planet Earth to clean toilets. Someday no one will be cleaning toilets—the robots will be doing that job. Move that stuff off your plate and get on with what you were really put on earth to do.

PARETO SUMMARY

▷ When you apply the Power Curve to time, you see that even a $20-per-hour person is worth $1,000 per hour at least one minute of every day.

▷ Your job, in managing your time, is to climb the Power Curve.

▷ As you climb the Power Curve, bigger opportunities always show up.

▷ Divide everything you do into $10-, $100-, and $1,000-per-hour tasks.

▷ As fast as possible, hire out the $10-per-hour tasks to others. Eventually you'll be delegating $100-per-hour tasks, too.

▷ Remember, basic household jobs are far easier to outsource than complex business tasks.

Make $1,000 Per Hour Doing What You Love

You want a marketing system that feeds you quality leads so that you spend your time only with customers who are ready to give you money.

Use Your Gifts: Focus on Your Talent Zone

It's not actually that hard to be worth $100 per hour. For the most part, you simply need to get *competent*. But to consistently be worth $1,000 or $10,000, you must be *excellent*.

You can be excellent in only so many areas. You need to build your excellence in the $1,000-per-hour and $10,000-per-hour jobs, not the $10-per-hour jobs. Some people are excellent at washing clothes, but washing clothes is never gonna pay the big bucks.

There are many tasks that you are *good* at, but they're not the highest value things you do. Let go. Pay someone else to do them. That's because . . .

Cold Prospecting and
Futzing Around with Websites =
Low-Paid Grunt Work

After consulting with thousands of entrepreneurs across 300+ industries, building my own team, and experiencing all kinds of challenges, I realized a tool was needed that could help each person know where to focus his skills. So I created the *Marketing DNA Test* to measure how you most naturally sell and persuade.

Go to www.perrymarshall.com/8020supplement, and access the Marketing DNA Test. In 10 to 15 minutes, it will report your unique profile, measuring eight different communication styles:

- **Alchemist.** How much **creativity and imagination** do you use to persuade?
- **Producer.** How much do you employ **systems and rules** when you persuade?
- **Live.** How naturally do you persuade **on the spot**?
- **Recorded.** Do you like to **refine and edit** in advance?
- **Images.** How much do you rely on **visual** elements to communicate?
- **Words.** How much do you prefer **written and verbal** communication?
- **Empathy.** How much **emotion** do you use to persuade?
- **Analytics.** How much do you count on **facts, numbers, and logic** when you persuade?

Here's the Marketing DNA Test result, for my friend Dave Frees, an attorney in Pennsylvania. Dave also speaks and writes on communication and persuasion for both sales and family relationships. Dave says this test, in Figure 16–1, on page 127, "nailed" him:

As you can see, Dave sells by leading with empathy—his emotional connection with the person he's with, by means of words. He does his best persuasion live, on the spot. He does not like to be analytical when he persuades; he dislikes "recorded," meaning he doesn't like to polish and perfect; he wants to just stand and deliver.

Figure 16–1. The Marketing DNA Test produces a report like this one that measures you on eight key aspects of persuasion.

Have other people on your team take the test, too. You'll see that people vary hugely in their natural communication styles.

This kind of information is critical when you're building your sales and marketing team. Persuasion happens in *all kinds* of different ways. Some people get in front of another person and negotiate face-to-face. Some people sell best by giving presentations to audiences.

Some people sell best by writing. Others with pictures. Others by studying best practices and following them; others by astounding customers with ingenuity. Some pluck heartstrings; others deliver cold, hard facts.

It is rare these days for one person to be able to successfully cover all the marketing bases—even in a small company in a small niche. Whatever you're good at, focus on—and make sure if you've got gaping holes, that you have people who can fill them.

Do this:

1. Invest heavily in building your strongest skills, and
2. Find other people to do everything else. Someone else is great at what you're bad at.

Before you hire anyone, have them take the Marketing DNA Test.

Most of us tend to hire people like ourselves. Alchemists like alchemists, producers like producers, writers like writers, and video people like video people. But every movie needs great writers, and every creative genius needs to be surrounded with people who can stick to a plan.

The Marketing DNA Test will generate a detailed report for you just like Dave's, plus a whole lot more. The test system will also send you a series of follow-up emails, which pinpoint items that the initial report couldn't cover, so you can further refine your efforts.

Know Thyself

I spent most of my 20s fighting my own nature. I was a multilevel marketing junkie, an engineer, and a sales rep. I was trying to be just like every superstar that I admired, killing myself in the process. For several years, my mantra was: "Massive action solves every problem!"

Which was just incredibly stupid, because "massive action" without a really great strategy gives you only more problems. Your efforts create work that is unfocused and dissipates your energy. I spent thousands of hours pounding the phone and busting down doors and battering brick walls with the tender skin of my nose.

I constantly put myself in situations where my greatest strengths got shoved in the closet, and my weaknesses were on display for all to see, all day long. I felt horribly inadequate, and my cumulative string of failures clung to my leg like a ball and chain.

At one point, I went to a church retreat about giftedness. We sat down and did a bunch of evaluations. The results said I should be doing totally different things than what I was *trying* to do.

I remember climbing into my green Toyota Tercel hatchback at the end of the retreat, sliding another motivational tape into my car radio, and muttering to myself, "Self, that's nice and all, but you can muscle your way through anything. If the dream is big enough, the facts don't count. Dude, keep the hammer down!"

Fast forward a couple of years . . . I'm on the brink of financial collapse and almost ready to crack on the inside. Each day I'm dragging around a ball and chain of failure and shame.

Then I get demoted to production manager from my sales rep job. I pull out my notebook from that retreat and say to myself, "Self, maybe you should take this seriously."

I did a *serious* self-inventory. I realized I had all kinds of skills I was ignoring, and I was trying to be someone I wasn't. My plan was not working. I decided to respect the test.

The Marketing DNA Test recognizes that everyone has to sell some time or another, even if they're not a salesperson. Everyone has to get a job. Everyone has to play patty-cake with bosses and committees. Everyone struggles to get their ideas accepted. It's not whether you *need* to persuade or whether you're trying; it's a question of *how* you persuade. Since you're in the business of persuading, you might as well persuade in the way that's most natural for you.

If you're a natural writer, you'll earn compound interest becoming a *better* writer. If you're an awesome amateur video producer, you'll earn compound interest building your video chops even more. If you thrive on presenting to live audiences, hone that skill to perfection.

By the way, one of the things in my notebook from that retreat said was, "You should be writing."

Writing? Whatever for? What would I write *about?* This made *no* sense to me at the time. I didn't believe there was any money to be made in writing at all. I didn't know there was an entire spectrum of selling opportunities that were fueled by writing (the entire direct-marketing industry!). I didn't even know what a copywriter was. I thought it was someone who mails registrations to the U.S. copyright and trademark office.

I'm sure one of the reasons I didn't know this was, that I had blinders on. But my very act of paying attention to that advice took the blinders off. Ever since, writing has grown into one of my personal selling tools.

Your gifts may be completely different from mine. But whatever they are, you need to find a selling environment that harnesses them to your maximum advantage.

Assignment: Unique Capability Survey

I'd like you to email five friends and colleagues who know you in different ways and from different walks of life. This is the "Unique Capability" survey. Choose people who have known you for at least five years.

Email them and say,

> Hi, I'm taking Perry Marshall's productivity course. You know me well, and one of the assignments is to ask:
>
> What is my unique capability?
>
> What do I naturally do better than most people?
>
> Please reply back with any thoughts you have. This really means a lot to me. Thanks.

Then when you get replies from your friends, sift and sort through their responses, and ask yourself:

- What talents did ALL of your friends mention?
- What talents did most of them mention?
- What talents did at least two of them mention?

This exercise indicates what you should be doing every day. You will also find this exercise encouraging and edifying, because most of us do not normally get a lot of positive feedback from other people. Mostly we just hear about our screw-ups, and it's more socially acceptable to give people "constructive criticism" than to praise them for their gifts.

But you can't build a successful career on your screw-ups or even by fixing your faults. You build a successful career *despite* your faults, by investing time, money, education, and practice into your gifts.

I'd like you to pull all of your friends' answers together and condense them into a single paragraph that describes what your "giftedness zone" is.

That, in combination with the Marketing DNA Test, will give you a clear idea of where you should be focusing your energy. I borrowed this Unique Capability exercise from Dan Sullivan of Strategic Coach, and it's one of the greatest things you will ever do for yourself. Not only should you do it, you should celebrate it, focus on it, and make sure that this time next year, you've invested in the gold that your friends called out in you.

Build on Your Team Members' Strengths

Ask the people on your business team to take the DNA test and the Unique Capability survey. Then get together, have everyone share the results, and give everyone a chance to elaborate on what they see in each other. Ask everyone what tasks they crave and what tasks they really don't want anymore. I guarantee you, it'll be one of the most fun, most productive get-togethers you've ever had.

The reason is, it's pretty unusual for people to plainly and openly praise one another for their strengths. I think people are somehow afraid it will go to the other person's head. It's actually more socially acceptable to nitpick and issue minor criticisms, to qualify any praise item with "And if you could just do ___ a little bit better next time," as though the goal were to balance positive with negative.

Think about it: Positive is just plain better. Sure, we need correction every now and then, but when somebody does a good job, they need to hear about it. We can only build on our strengths. Make calling out other peoples' strengths a value in your company culture, and everyone will love working for you.

Everyone's Unique Capability Is Different

The beauty of bringing 80/20 to a team is that it honors peoples' giftedness. If you have 30 kids in a classroom, one of them has vastly more ability in math than the others. Another's passion is science. Another is into martial arts. Another is fascinated with beats and music mashups. Another plays the violin. Another loves sewing. Another plays basketball. When you stop trying to make everyone the same, their true passions and abilities shine.

Love List, Hate List

Your Unique Capability survey, together with some of the other things you love to do and know you're good at, form your **Love List.** You need to be clear about what you want to be doing every day.

You also need a Hate List.

Your Hate List is things you're not good at, don't enjoy, drag you down, confuse you, waste time, embarrass you.

Just in case you're interested, here's my Hate List:

- Administration
- Paperwork
- Politics
- Petty arguments
- Criticizing. I hate criticizing people. It's not me. It's not what I like to do.
- Micro-managing. I couldn't micro-manage anyone else to save my life.

Please notice: Some people are *great* at all these things. Some people love all those things. My wife is a great administrator. My personal assistant and my CPA are fast and efficient with paperwork. Some folks are brilliant at navigating politics, and everybody's got a relative who loves to argue about anything and everything at Thanksgiving dinner—the pettier, the better.

Some people are professional critics (they trash bad movies and relish every minute of it), and some people micro-manage everything and everyone in their life.

When you put *any* of those people in the *right* role, they shine. Whatever it is that you hate to do, somebody else loves to do it. Define your Hate List, right now, and give somebody else a job. They will thank you for it.

PARETO SUMMARY

▷ Score yourself with the Marketing DNA Test. Gain free access at www.perrymarshall.com/8020supplement/.

▷ Email five people who know you well, and ask them what your Unique Capability is.

▷ Develop your Love List and Hate List, and remember—anything you hate to do, somebody else loves doing it.

17

80/20 Hiring and Outsourcing

It's Not an Interview, It's an Audition!

R ecently seen on Twitter:

> Ken McCarthy (@KenMcCarthy)
> Help Wanted: Someone to deal with all the stupid people in the world so I don't have to anymore. Name your price.

You go out next week and hire 10 salespeople. All of them work for you for a few months. Almost inevitably, here's how the 10 of them are going to stack up after they've had a chance to generate some sales. Let's assume the 10 generated a total of $300,000 of sales last month. Here's how they're almost certainly going to stack up:

1. Karen $91,500
2. Scott $50,300
3. Bill $35,500

4. Regina $27,700
5. Marilyn $22,900
6. Greg $19,500
7. Steve $17,100
8. Sunil $15,200
9. Mark $0
10. Evan $0

I got the top eight numbers from the tool at www.8020curve.com. But I figured you've always got two who are complete duds, so in my chart, Mark and Evan at the bottom got goose eggs.

Since sales is so crucial to a business, it's imperative that you hire salespeople with an **audition** instead of an **interview**, because the laws of the universe say it's almost impossible for the top two to *not* create more than half the results.

What applicants *say* to you at the interview probably has little relation to their capability. What they actually *do* when you take them out on a test drive is far more reliable.

If you hire salespeople one at a time and nurture them slowly, you have only a 1-in-10 chance of finding Karen the first time out. It's actually worse than that, because if Karen's any good she's already working for someone, and she's probably not surfing the job boards. It's real easy to go through 20 duds if you just take whoever shows up.

It would take two years to go through these 10. Actually, you should try out all of them in two months.

Yes, I know, this seems very *Darwinian*. But in the long run, the cruelest thing you can do to yourself *or* any salesperson is live in the "should be" world instead of living in the "is" world. You just need to set up expectations in advance.

When you evaluate them, you make it very clear: "We're going to try you out for . . ." however long it takes for them to prove their worth. Three days, three weeks, three months—however long it takes. Explain to them that they're not truly hired until the evaluation period is over. Tell them: "Welcome to your test drive. Yes, we will pay you, but this is just a *test drive*."

And before you even get that far, give them something to do right away. "Here's 50 old sales leads. Call these people and find at least one 'live' one in the bunch and pass it back to me." Give 50 leads to 5 salespeople and you're going to learn a lot about them real fast.

They don't even have to be on the payroll yet. Maybe you just pay them 100 bucks to spend a morning or afternoon in your office.

Sales Funnel in Reverse

When you build a sales funnel—whether you're selling toys or $500,000 software packages—you're creating a system that sells you to your customer in a series of steps.

The audition process for hiring is really just a reverse sales funnel. Since the people you're hiring don't have a process for evaluating you, you create the process for evaluating them. The Power Triangle still applies—Traffic—Conversion—Economics—but it's them convincing you they're worth the money.

The Five Power Disqualifiers also apply:

1. *Money*. Will they work for what you're willing to pay?
2. *Bleeding Neck*. Do they want a change of scenery in their career right away?
3. *USP*. Do they bring special skills to your team?
4. *Do they have the ability to say yes and accept the job?* (Maybe they're just using you to get a raise.)
5. *Does working at your company fit into the overall plans for themselves and their family?*

Sourcing Workers Online

You can do the same thing with writers, web designers, and programmers: Give them something to *do*. So let's talk about hiring other people. We'll start with remote online outsourcing through services like oDesk, Elance, and Fiverr.

There are a few fantasies about outsourcing work that are entertained in online marketing:

1. "All you need is a bunch of people on Elance who will work real cheap for ya."

2. "You don't want employees or staff; all they'll do is irritate you. You can be a one-man band with a virtual assistant."

3. "Whatever you do, you don't want a bunch of employees."

There's truth in all those fantasies. There are also problems with all of them.

First, you CAN get great talent at places like Elance.com and Guru.com. But the 80/20 rule ALWAYS applies. Never assume you can find serious talent without serious disqualification. You want top 4 percent, top 1 percent players.

How to Hire Great Talent Online

Start with the easy stuff: Talent sites like Elance.com or Fiverr.com. You can post $50 or $500 projects on Elance, and there's not much damage if something goes wrong. Fiverr is even easier—pay the five bucks, post your request, and away you go.

The greatest virtue of these services is that the threat of a bad user rating does much to increase the quality of the work. If somebody's done 50 projects in the same category, and they have a 9.0 out of 10 rating, then you can be sure they're pretty good. Tips:

- If you post a bid, offer a reasonable price, and pick someone with a good rating, you still have a 50 percent chance of a botched project. Choose two bidders, and pay them both to do it.

- Go for the top 1 percent: Find the "Top 100 coders" or "Top 100 workers" list, and privately bid your project directly to that worker. He's got a 9.7 average rating over a span of 63 projects, and a 6.0 rating would kill him. He'll drive through walls to deliver a good product, and he's naturally, inherently gifted.

- Do a small project with a bidder before commencing a large one. Fiverr is great for this. You can spend $100, hand out micro projects to 20 people in one hour, and within a few days you've auditioned 20 people with an almost foolproof indication of how good they are. Fiverr is the fastest way in history to rack the shotgun.

Managing Subcontractors

If you have 10 different projects going with all these subcontractors all over the world, you now have a full-time project management job on your hands, which is fine if you're a great project manager. (I am not.) Eventually you need someone you can completely trust, and who is under your complete control, to do this for you. I believe that talent needs to be in-house. So how do you hire people?

I've done a lot of it lately, and I applied 80/20 all the way. It began when I decided to contract an Affiliate Manager and a Content Czar. I posted descriptions for each (these examples are instructive; search perrymarshall.com for "affiliate manager" and "content czar," and you can see the announcements on my blog).

I told my customer service manager, Jeremy, to do all the frontline screening. So he wouldn't get deluged with junk, we added a disqualifier: a $25 application fee.

A bunch of people complained loudly and . . . immediately disqualified themselves.

I got 12 Affiliate applications and 19 Content Czar applications. Almost all of them were at least respectable. *The $25 fee weeded out everyone who didn't think they could win.* I eliminated all but five Affiliate apps and nine CZ apps and then gave them an assignment. To the Affiliate applicants, I created a sales audition. I told them, "You've got a week. Put together some deals, and show me what you can do." Two produced results, three did not. One produced far more than the others and that was Jack Born.

I told the nine CZ applicants to take the MP3s, transcripts, handouts ,and supplemental material for one of my training programs plus detailed results of a customer survey and create a mini-product that I can sell for 20 to 40 bucks. They had to package the product and write the sales promotion, and I'd pay them a commission on any sales.

I got four products I deemed worthy. Joshua won and became the new Content Czar. There was no way anybody could fake their way through this exercise.

Jack was both a salesman and a talented programmer—a rare blend of talents. Joshua, a copywriter, a speaker, and a salesman with ambition to burn. Both high-integrity, A-player guys.

It takes a team, and there's nothing like having a great one. Your mission, should you choose to accept it: Stop doing interviews; get to the truth quickly with auditions; judge people by what they do and not what they say; and build yourself a world-class team.

PARETO SUMMARY

▷ Since 80/20 applies to salespeople, you want to sort through them as fast as possible.
▷ Bring them on board on a trial basis before hiring them.
▷ Hiring should be an audition, not an interview.
▷ You can get all kinds of great help from online reverse-auction services like Elance, but you must rack the shotgun to screen out the bad ones.

How to Get More $1,000/Hour Work Done with a Personal Assistant

The easiest way to get a fast productivity boost is to hire someone whose job is to do "anything I don't want to do."

Initially that might even be the job description. Your Personal Assistant (PA) should read this book and understand that his or her job is whatever 80 percent of your work that you don't want to do.

As jobs go, this is not a particularly bad job. Some days it's downright adventurous. When I was in college working on assembly lines, I would have relished being some executive or entrepreneur's errand boy. And I'd have learned a great deal in the process. Would've been way better than flipping burgers or stocking shelves in a warehouse.

Everyone whose time is worth more than about $30 per hour should consider getting someone like this. It doesn't have to be an "errand boy" or "girl Friday." It could be a housekeeper, a cook, or a handyman. But the reason a PA is so good is, he or she can hire all those other people! I learned from my friend Scott Tucker. He told his assistant: "Don't bring me questions. Bring me answers."

If you want to join a band, do you have a big long conversation about all the gigs you've played and what you think about David Bowie?

No. They ask you to bring your bass and play. Audition.

In my business—and in most online businesses—excellent written and communication skills are extremely important. So when we want to hire someone, the advertisement says:

"Wanted: XYZ type person who will do ABC type work for JKL type company. Do not send resume; write us a letter in Microsoft Word format, explaining why we should hire you. Email to xyzapplications@ gmail.com."

You can thin the herd considerably by asking them to FAX it to you.

Three-fourths of applicants will fail to follow the instructions. They'll put the doc in PDF, write it in an email with no attachment, or attach a resume. They're all instantly disqualified.

One out of two or three who follows the instructions will probably impress you with his or her letter. Next, tell them to call you at a very specific time, like 10:15 A.M. on Tuesday.

If they call at 10:22, they're disqualified.

You will quickly be surprised at how few people can follow simple instructions. You'll find that you have to spend more money advertising the position simply because the applications are so lame. Only those who call at 10:15 even get to talk to you.

Notice that prior to this point you have only had to read maybe two to four letters, and that's it. Nothing else.

At this point you have effectively thinned 20 would-be resumes down to one conversation with a person who has already impressed you. This is a sales funnel in reverse. They have to sell you; they have to jump through your hoops. If the phone interview goes well, set up an in-person interview. Again they have to show up on time, etc.

Early on, give them a Marketing DNA Test, which is a very useful qualification tool. This will give you a fairly accurate idea of their biases in communicating. It's usually best if you and your PA don't have the same work style.

If possible, give them a preliminary assignment. Maybe they can do some virtual work, and you can see how well they do. When I hired Jeremy I asked him to find me a rare book.

You will be surprised (shocked, actually) at how few people can follow simple instructions. You will be amazed that it's even possible for any country to have an unemployment rate of *less* than 10 percent.

Again, when you hire them, hire them on a trial basis. "We're going to go for two weeks and see how things go. After that you're officially on the payroll, if you pass."

Your PA must be extremely trustworthy and respect confidentiality. He or she can't be emotionally dependent or need to involve themselves in your personal dramas. This is *very* important. You cannot afford to be emotionally entangled with your staff.

Several people I know have had to go through four or five people before they found a PA who was really good. But believe me, it's worth the trouble. A good PA will save you 30 hours per week and clear your plate for bigger, better, more lucrative opportunities.

My PA, Lorena, was a friend of a friend. I knew she was looking for work so I initially hired her just to do stuff around the house and run errands, like changing furnace filters and taking the car to the mechanic. Little by little I started giving her more complex assignments.

Lorena handles a LOT of niggling details—putting things in my calendar, setting up phone calls, confirming appointments, checking schedules, sending emails, making travel arrangements, hiring out various tasks— things most people naturally do for themselves without question. Every day, it adds up to hours of $10-per-hour work that would drain my energy.

My staff knows my time is way too valuable for me to be doing stuff they could be doing instead. They also know my time is too valuable to just sit around and shoot the bull. But it doesn't keep us from having fun. When we have fun, we're deliberate about it. We work hard, and we play hard.

It is *normal* to feel uncomfortable and even guilty about making other people do stuff you *could* do. But it's the only way you can outgrow the limitations of your current time constraints.

It's OK to only do stuff you want to do! It's OK to take a vacation day while your employees work for you.

Why? Because: House cleaners want a job. Lawn services want a job. The kid down the street wants to shovel or rake for some extra money. Your PA wants a job. Give them the stuff you don't want.

If you are doing this right, you will discover that an entire ecosystem has been built around you, and it's possible because you have created space where you can do several hours of $1,000/hour work every single day.

Sometimes your PA may pick up your kids from soccer practice, buy gifts for your kids or spouse, whatever. That's fine.

Obviously you can take this too far. No one is above taking out the trash. (Sam Walton even insisted that every executive at Walmart, no matter how high up in the company, empty his own trashcan. Sam also drove a pickup truck.) Your family needs your involvement. You don't want them to feel like they're just another "outsourced project." I have occasionally made the mistake of erring in that direction.

The Power of a Great Personal Assistant

I have a friend, Bill, who ran a large trade organization with hundreds of member companies. Bill organized several national conferences per year, worked with trade magazines and trade shows, and oversaw several standards committees. Over a period of a couple of years I watched Bill bring a hot new technology that nobody had ever heard of to national prominence.

I was surprised to learn that the entire firm consisted of Bill, his PA, Patti, and just a couple of part-time support staff. Man, did these guys have a big footprint for such a small organization. Bill's group had a lot of moving parts. Bill was the idea guy, spokesman, and salesman. But Patti was the reason the operation ran like a well-oiled machine. It became clear that Patty was the real "man behind the curtain."

Later, Bill left to start a new trade organization in a different industry. He took Patti with him.

Patti was absolutely crucial to Bill's success. She might have started out at $10 per hour for all I know. But in time she became a well-compensated, crucial team player.

Your PA Is Your Translator

I have a friend who lived in Ukraine for nine months. He didn't speak Ukrainian, so he had to hire a translator. He quickly discovered that in a foreign country, your translator becomes your closest confidant. If your translator lies to you or misrepresents you or the people you're talking to, you are totally screwed. It may take you a long time to figure out what's really going on. And in all likelihood, you'll never find out exactly what happened. You'll just know it was a disaster.

A high-power PA is a lot like that translator. He or she knows your world in detail and thinks and acts on your behalf. His or her performance is critical.

80/20 says that as soon as you achieve some level of success, you should have a gatekeeper. But don't isolate yourself in concrete walls.

Once I was dealing with a company owned by a woman with whom I was somewhat acquainted. Her customer service person was *extremely* rude—"I can't believe what this person just said to me" rude.

So I tried to email her, but her rude employee intercepted the email. I tried to fax, but the fax never reached her. I couldn't call because her gatekeeper got all the phone calls. Finally I gave up because I didn't have her cell phone or home address, and I couldn't figure out a way to penetrate her fortress.

A year later I bumped into her at a conference and told her all about it. She was appalled. There had been other problems, too—there always are.

Don't let this happen to you.

If you delegate your work properly, with systems for quality control, you will have time to make a $500,000 income *and* spend time with your family, and your life will be less stressful than it was when you made only $100K.

Not only that, most people's "Quantum Leaps" in business are closely associated with making these kinds of changes—not just marketing breakthroughs but breakthroughs in delegation.

PARETO SUMMARY

▷ Everyone who makes more than $30 per hour should have a Personal Assistant. Even if you're an employee, you should hire one out of your own pocket. You'll come out way ahead.

▷ Your PA can do just about anything for you and easily save you 10 hours per week.

▷ You'll probably have to try out a few people before you find a good match.

▷ Make sure the person you hire respects confidentiality and doesn't have "boundary issues" with you.

▷ A high-power PA will become one of your most mission-critical team members.

Fire the Bottom 10 Percent!

O ne of the most popular emails I've ever sent was this one:

SUBJECT LINE: Sometimes You've Just Gotta FIRE a Customer

Jack Welch, who led GE to blazing success, had a rule: You gotta get rid of the bottom 10 percent your employees every year. Controversial, but it obviously worked.

I say, the same applies to customers. The worst of them are NOT worth it. And in today's email we celebrate the firing of one of MY customers. This one's a case study in "jerk factor."

This guy (we'll call him "A") registered for the $95 application fee to come to the seminar, but his credit card didn't go through. Then when Jeremy contacted "A" to straighten this out, "A" started demanding to be given a whole bunch of information (almost all of which was already on the sales letter BTW!), and then he just got nasty:

"If the seminar isn't good or is just a sales pitch or is a bunch of eager yahoos all running forward to lick boots and ingratiate themselves like whining curs, frankly I'd rather sit tight where I am."

"I could deliver a two-hours speech on AdWords and 25 percent click-through ratios in the toughest industries out there at 5¢/click."

"Your reticence to give me the information (basic: schedule and accommodations) and eagerness to whack my card non-refundable fees has me very, very wary of your entire organization at this point. Most of the goodwill that the *Definitive Guide to Google AdWords* created is down the drain."

Jeremy spent an entire week trying to be nice to this guy. (The application fee IS refundable, and the details are on my site. But you have to understand Jeremy—he's just about the nicest guy you can find.

All this was going on without my knowledge. But when I saw his email, I snapped.

I wrote him back:

"You are not invited to this seminar; all further discussion about this is terminated, and also I am terminating your membership. I will not tolerate having my employees being treated the way you have been treating Jeremy, especially when you refuse to pay. I am sorry for any misunderstanding, but I expect my members to use good etiquette with our staff at all times."

People like "A" do not belong at my seminar. They do not belong on my customer list. They do not belong on YOUR customer list. People like "A" need to be fired. They eat up time, resources, and emotional energy better devoted to customers who treat you and your employees right.

YOU have customers like this, too (right?), and truth be told, you can see 'em coming a mile away. The only thing that makes them happy is when they get their pound of flesh out of somebody.

I'm giving you permission to fire them. Get rid of 'em. Cancel their purchase order, give 'em their money back, send 'em packing. Then give your precious time and attention to another customer who deserves it. The one who deserves it is almost always less demanding, doesn't have this nasty entitlement complex, and spends money with you, with less resistance.

The best-paying customers are also usually the ones that treat you with the most respect. You get the best of both worlds—or the worst. You decide. I don't care how much you think you need the business, you don't want it from "A." Get rid of him. He's easily replaced.

Make it your Friday celebration today. Do it before noon and celebrate at lunch time!

Happy Firing,

Perry Marshall

P.S. Got a great "I fired a customer" story? Reply and send it to us. I'll compile them and let everyone in on the fun.

Man did I get a TON of emails. Probably over 100 stories. You can get them in the online book supplement in the member's area at www.perrymarshall.com/8020supplement/. Several are very eye-opening, and a number offer great insights on how to navigate tricky situations.

One of the best ways to move energy and resources from the bottom of the Power Curve to the top is to fire a customer. You don't have to be mean about it; you can just say, "we've reviewed our accounts, and it just doesn't make sense for us to do business anymore."

Yes, You've Gotta Fire the Bottom 10 Percent of Employees, Too

I HATE firing people.

I've had to do it several times, and I always cringe. But it must be done. I know this, because I've been fired myself from at least five different jobs.

The odds are overwhelming that the bottom 10 percent of your organization is performing at far below its potential and seriously holding you back. You need to let them go.

And you already know who it is.

In my experience, it's not usually that they're "bad people." It's more like the job just doesn't fit them, or maybe they've grown bored with it.

That bottom 10 percent is sucking up time and energy. It's generating negativity. It's breeding incompetence. Your customers are not being treated right. Your other employees are not being served well. Some of your peeps are creating more problems than they solve.

If firing someone is so painful for you that you're tempted to just not do it, then offer them a nice fat severance package. It's costing you more money to have them on board than it'll cost to pay their severance or unemployment.

Just do what you need to do. Replace the under performer with a top performer. And do everything you can to point the exiting person in a better direction.

I'm thankful for every one of the five times I got fired. When I got laid off from my acoustical engineering job, I went into sales, which was initially tough but ultimately far more rewarding. When I got fired from my manufacturer's rep job, it was because I was trying to force a square peg into a round hole. I was so persistent, I would have kept going maybe for years if my boss Wally hadn't called the whole thing to a halt.

Someday the person you fire will thank you for it, too.

If you don't enforce high standards for your employees—and expect them to comply—then what kind of employee are you creating for the next employer?

Nobody benefits when you or I subsidize incompetence and sloppy standards. *Nobody.* The pursuit of excellence and quality, and the keeping of promises and deadlines, are the only things that keep the civilized world humming along. Everything else is destructive. This applies to your employees, your vendors, your joint venture partners—everyone who gets money from you.

My customers expect excellence from me, my employees expect their paychecks on time, and I'm going to expect the same from them. You should, too.

Yes, There Is Room in the World for Cutting People Some Slack . . .

When my daughter Tannah was five, she took cello lessons. One Sunday afternoon, we attended her music recital. All the teacher's students were playing their pieces for the parents, and a 10-year-old girl with Down syndrome methodically pecked out a rendition of "The First Noel" on the piano.

She received hearty applause from everyone. Why? Not because she's a musical virtuoso, but because she did her best. She embraced excellence to the best of her ability, and she deserves the applause.

We can't expect *everyone* to be virtuosos. But we *must* expect everyone to do what they're capable of doing.

When ordinary people do what they're really capable of, they're proud of their accomplishments and the door is opened to more accomplishment. There is a place in the world for charity. But subsidizing mediocrity is not charity.

Violate "Something for Nothing" . . . and Pay the Consequences

You end up paying by squandering valuable resources. Your customers *also* pay a price because those resources—including your valuable time—aren't being spent on helping them.

On the other hand, when you set expectations and make people meet them, everyone benefits thrice. The employee benefits from the discipline, and you benefit from the work that gets done. So do your customers.

PARETO SUMMARY

▷ You do yourself no favors by keeping toxic customers around.
▷ You do employees no favors by tolerating lousy performance.
▷ Fire your problem customers.
▷ Fire the bottom 10 percent of your employees.

80/20 Controversy
Get Famous by Polarizing Your Market

8 0/20 says that you and I must *always* design mechanisms into our advertising that segments our prospects into categories:

1. Not interested
2. Mildly interested
3. Interested . . . hopefully soon
4. Interested right now
5. Extremely interested
6. Fascinated and transfixed
7. Insanely obsessed and addicted

Of course, lead generation eliminates the people at stage 1 or 2 and leaves you with the rest, making your job as a salesperson much easier. But the real profits come as you cultivate people at levels 5, 6, and 7. They're much easier and less expensive to sell to.

But there's a whole 'nother dimension to this, which is when those seven categories describe not only how much people *love* you—but how much they *hate* you.

The Amazon.com "Three-Star-Rating" Phenomenon of Hyper-Responsive, Rabid Markets

There's a very interesting, very instructive phenomenon that occurs in many markets and walks of life. If it exists in your market, you're a fool not to harness it. The easiest place to observe it is in the book reviews on Amazon.

Let's pick a controversial book. Hillary Clinton's *It Takes A Village* is a great example. People either love her or hate her. Rarely is anyone neutral about Hillary Clinton.

Almost all books on highly controversial topics, or books written by or about controversial people, have average ratings of **three stars,** but *hardly any actual three-star ratings*. All of the reviews are either **one star** or **five stars.**

Hillary's book *It Takes a Village* is in fact a perfect case study (see Figure 20–1).

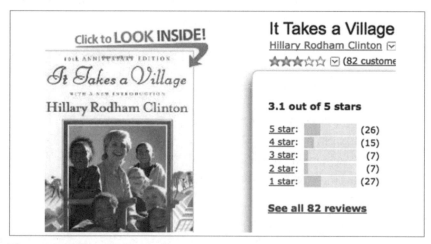

Figure 20–1. Highly polarizing books have lots of five-star ratings and lots of one-star ratings, and hardly any three-stars.

See the lots of five stars/one star profile on the number of reviews? That is two 80/20 curves back to back. One is forward; the other is backward. So your market actually looks like Figure 20–2.

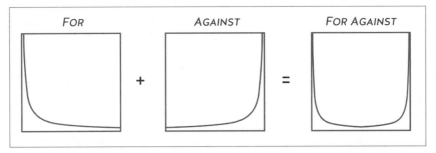

Figure 20–2. The "80/20 Saddle Curve" is when your market is driven by two groups: Those FOR, and those AGAINST. You get two 80/20 curves back to back, representing two levers. Almost all the controversy is fueled by a small minority of the hyper-extremes. (Illustration by Danielle Flanagan.)

I call this the 80/20 Saddle Curve. You are really dealing with *two* 20 percents, two groups of hyper-responsive buyers: People who love you, people who hate you. Two top 5 percents, two top 1 percents.

You clearly see this in any controversial topic: Liberals vs. conservatives, Democrats vs. Republicans, pro-life vs. pro-choice, creation vs. evolution, union vs. anti-union.

In all these scenarios, two small, highly polarized groups of people control the majority of a conversation. The entire landscape is dominated by those two sides. Eric Hoffer, in his incredibly insightful book, *The True Believer,* said, "The game of history is usually played by the best and the worst over the heads of the majority in the middle."

This is hugely important in politics, shaping public policies, and elections, because *the apathetic middle doesn't matter.* They don't care enough to make their voice heard. In an election, they don't vote.

In an election, the extreme 5 percent on each side is not going to change. Hard-core conservatives are going to vote conservative; hard-core liberals are going to vote liberal. Very little will change that.

The middle is not going to show up at the polls and cast a vote, either. So the election is really swung one way or the other by the *moderately interested* left and the *moderately interested right*. This is a major component of any campaign strategy.

In fact, I did an entire interview about this regarding the U.S. 2012 election and the battle between Barack Obama and Mitt Romney. It vividly shows what Obama did differently than Romney, and why Obama won—in an economic climate that was favorable in many ways to Romney. You can access that at www.perrymarshall.com/8020supplement.

The 80/20 Saddle Curve makes it simple and easy to see what's really going on in a power struggle between opposing sides. This applies in *any* market that's prone to controversy. And what market is there with no controversy? It could be arguments about children's immunization, participation in the European Union, PC vs. Mac, cotton vs. polyester, anything.

No matter what market you are in, there's a controversy about something. The fastest, easiest way to become famous is to pick a side that you're passionate about and start advocating. This is the straightest path to selling books, but if you sell, say, equipment, there are always controversies in an industry about how it should be used.

If you take a definite position, you're quotable. If you're quotable, magazine editors quote you. Then you get invited to be on panels at conferences. People see you in public, and it's always easier to close a sale when you're a mini-celebrity.

So, for example, this means that there's two kinds of blog posts:

1. The "everybody's on the same side" blog post, with 500 comments from 498 people. (Two of them commented twice.)
2. The "for-against" blog post. It's got 500 comments from 50 people. 400 of the comments are from five people—two for, three against—and they've been arguing back and forth with each other in your comment section for two weeks.

These two examples pretty much sum up peoples' opinions about this book. Sometimes the reviews are rebuttals to other reviews, so Amazon's review sections become a place for ferocious debate between people on two sides of a particular spectrum. The 80/20 Saddle Curve is right there in the review summary. All we have to do is turn it on its side, as in Figure 20–4, page 157.

⭐⭐⭐⭐⭐ **careful, caring and not communist**

⭐☆☆☆☆ **Typical Leftist Bromides**

Figure 20–3. The Amazon reviews of Hillary Clinton's book are quintessential examples of for-against.

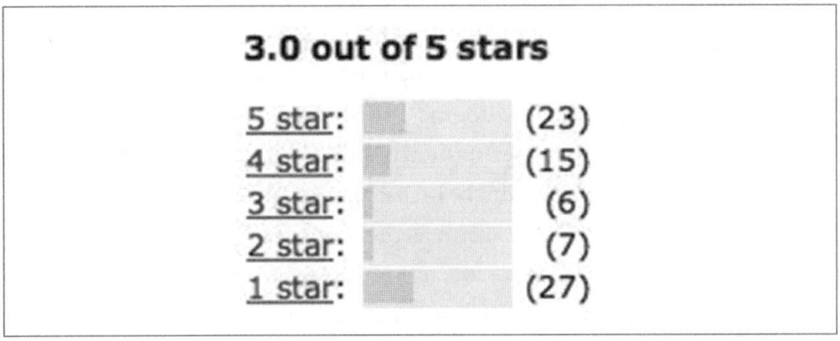

3.0 out of 5 stars

5 star: (23)
4 star: (15)
3 star: (6)
2 star: (7)
1 star: (27)

Figure 20–4. Amazon stars flipped on their side perfectly illustrate the 80/20 Saddle Curve.

There's a potent marketing lesson here. Who buys a book like *It Takes a Village*? Who reads it? Two kinds of people:

1. People who love Hillary

2. People who hate her guts

Those are the only two kinds of people who matter. Most political and social battles are fought by the people on the extremes. They are the only ones who speak out, and the only ones who really even pay attention to Hillary at all.

The beauty of this is, you get to collect *dinero* from folks on both sides of the aisle.

Now, of course, the ones who hate Hillary are only going to give money for the book—they're not going to support her election. So she has to pander to the crowd that loves her dearly. But do not miss the fact that a significant portion of Hillary's book buyers was people who can't stand her.

If you want to get love and adoration from raving fans, you almost certainly need to be willing to be reviled by others. If you are not willing to take a stand, you are boring. You are milquetoast. You have nothing interesting to say.

You learn to recognize those hyper-responsive people when you see them. You want to know how they walk and how they talk, because when you're successful you'll probably be appealing to one end of some spectrum, and profiting from the rabid 5 percent:

- **They're extremely emotional, to the point of being irrational.** Regardless of HOW wrong or right they may be, they won't entertain any possible merits of the other side. The most fanatical people on each extreme enjoy insulting their opponents and calling people ugly names. They love dogma and slogans.
- **The fastest way to permanently bond with a Hillary Hater is to say something deliciously insulting about Hillary.** Tell an excruciating Hillary joke. As soon as the words escape your lips, this person will feel an intense attraction toward you. They will suddenly want to buy something from you. They may invite you over to their house for dinner. They might ask you on a date.
- **There's nothing more powerful than selling against an enemy.** The existence of a common enemy creates a market. If this sounds strange to you, remember how much Osama Bin Laden toilet paper got sold after September 11, 2001.

- **There are two sides to every argument.** My friend Howie Jacobson grew up in the home of a labor leader, and the slogan he heard growing up was "Up with the Wages, Down with the Bosses." He can still sing three verses of "Solidarity Forever" and the entire song "Union Maid" by Woody Guthrie. It was only much later that he saw that there might be such a thing as bad employees.

    I had the opposite experience: I used to think labor unions were evil. It was only after I and three other salespeople had to unanimously threaten to quit to get a vile, wicked human being out of our sales department that I realized that upper management can be quite clueless at times—and yes, abusive, too.

- **The dark side of all of this is that it's hard to sell sanity and reason.** It's much easier to sell fanaticism and reactionary behavior. However . . . if you do sell slogans and if you bond with your audience via a mutual enemy, do us all a favor and package some sanity and clear thinking with it, somewhere. Please. I think it's your moral and social obligation to do so.

- **The best rallying point for your own cause or position in the marketplace is strong opposition.**

Immediately after the Newtown, Connecticut, shooting, anti-gun arguments flared up and sales of firearms skyrocketed. One of my friends, a gun enthusiast, showed me one of his fave websites where almost every gun was out of stock. He said the website had been down on and off for days at a time because it was besieged with so much business. *U.S. News and World Report* says the National Rifle Association got 250,000 new members in the month after the shooting.

Nothing puts more money in the gun industry's coffers than fierce protests against guns. Thus the old adage, "There's no such thing as bad publicity."

The position you take in your industry about how chiropractic care is done or how audio systems should be installed may not be as primal as guns, but when you take that position and beat the drum, you build a powerful publicity platform. You harness your opponent's energy to catapult you to stardom.

As a guy with an engineering degree, it took me a long, long time to get accustomed to the erratic, emotional nature of people and markets. I wanted people to do things for *rational reasons. Facts. Superior arguments. Better logic.* Still do. But that's not how people are, and that's not usually the most effective way to deal with people.

There's a hidden advantage to this irrational side of human nature, though: If you reach people at an emotional level, you can avoid having the argument in the first place.

Remaining Polarized vs. Stepping into No-Man's Land

Most of the time, opponents mischaracterize the other side, willfully misunderstand them, dehumanize, and demonize them. Sometimes a conservative has almost no liberal friends and a liberal has almost no conservative friends. Eventually they start to think such friendships would even be ridiculous and unnecessary. After all, the other guys are "just plain wrong."

Sometimes it's worse than that. Sometimes people on Side B get labeled as "imbeciles" and "idiots" and "morons." Leaders of Side A become so arrogant that they don't even bother to learn what Side B's position actually is. Have you ever gone to a live debate, expecting a headliner match, only to find that one side had not done their homework?

I admit it is politically useful; you can "win" without ever really understanding your opponent. But it's immature and lazy and perpetuates prejudice. The mature path is to recognize that the other side, no matter how much you might despise them, always has at least *some* legitimate reasons for feeling the way they feel.

- **The best way to get respect from your tribe is when your opposition cannot help but respect you.** That's only possible when you know thy enemy.
- **Triggering panic on the opposite side is the fastest way to raise your profile.** When your enemies talk about you—and explode into tirades about you—your allies can't help but overhear. It proves you're a force to be reckoned with.

How do you trigger panic? You address the issue at a higher level:

- If something on your side is broken and has frequently failed, stop pretending everything's OK and slapping bandages on the problem. Fix the problem at its core foundations, and prove that it works.
- If your opponents think you're full of it, then create a demonstration, a guarantee, a piece of inarguable evidence that definitively *proves* what you're saying is true.
- Expose a weakness that no one knows your opponent has.
- Lay down the gauntlet by offering an award or prize. For years, people thought that only governments could make spacecraft. Peter Diamandis created the $10-million X-Prize for spacecraft in 1996; then in 2004, a spaceship made two successful trips in two weeks, forever proving that private industry could produce manned trips into space.

If you're really serious about taking on the other side, begin by immersing yourself in their world so thoroughly that you can pretend to be one of them on command. Bryan Caplan, a professor of economics, coined the term "Ideological Turing Test."

A Turing Test is a machine intelligence contest where a human chats with a computer program. The goal is for the human to be fooled into thinking the machine is really another human.

The Ideological Turing Test is when you argue *for* the side you normally oppose and successfully convince everyone watching that you're actually "one of them." This is the acid test of knowing your competition. If you're a Democrat, can you convincingly sound like a Republican? Enough to convince Democrats that you're the real deal? Enough to convince other Republicans?

This is far more than an interesting exercise. When dialogue between two sides is stuck, with the same barbs being exchanged for the last 20 years, a breakthrough and a new conversation will probably come only from an outsider who brings fresh ideas to the table and is willing to go deep to understand both sides.

Usually, somewhere hides a solution that would make a lot of people on both sides happy. There is a huge opportunity in that solution. When you do that, you permanently shift the market.

This is what Gandhi did in his nonviolent protest of the British occupation of India. He understood that what people really wanted was peace, not war. People on both sides wanted this; it's just that most people couldn't see a way to accomplish this without shooting someone.

Gandhi had reason to believe the British would respect a nonviolent approach. His unique approach dissolved a long-standing conflict.

PARETO SUMMARY

▷ In highly polarized markets, you have a saddle curve: two 80/20 curves mirroring each other, back to back.

▷ The vocal minority dominates the apathetic majority.

▷ You can achieve rapid attention and stardom by triggering panic in the top 1 percent of your opposition.

▷ The only way to solve the conflict at its core is to deeply understand both sides.

CHAPTER

21

80/20 Market Research in a Single Afternoon

The most painful mistake any entrepreneur or salesperson makes is jumping into a swimming pool that has no water in it: namely, trying to sell something that nobody wants to buy.

Man, have I ever made that mistake. A whole bunch of times. I *still* make it sometimes.

One of the cardinal rules of marketing is: *Never go into a market unless you can write a page of your customer's diary and be so spooky-accurate that they wonder: "Hey were you spying on me last night?"*

When you can do that, your odds of success go up exponentially.

Before you dive into the pool, before you develop a product, before you create a brand, build a website, hire employees, or print 5,000 brochures, you need to find out if people want what you've got. You also need to get to a point where you can write a page of their diary.

The best person I know on this topic is Dr. Glenn Livingston. Glenn has been paid millions of dollars by large companies to do research; in fact, he's the guy who created the company name "Nextel." He did it with a special research method. When he left the corporate scene to be a solo entrepreneur, he brought his research techniques to the online marketing space.

Normally, the success rate of a new business is 10 to 20 percent. Glenn's methods bring that number to 50 percent, 75 percent, even 95 percent. I've seen Glenn plunge into markets over and over again, successfully—markets that he previously knew *nothing* about—and earn a nice profit.

In this chapter, guest-written by Glenn Livingston, he gives you the highlights of his success formula. Ignore this at your extreme peril.

How to Get $250,000 of Critical Market Data for Free with Nothing More Than Your Computer, an Internet Connection, and a Lazy Sunday Afternoon to Spare!
by Glenn Livingston, Ph.D.

What if I told you it were possible to get the same critical insights large companies used to pay professional research firms a quarter-million dollars for—in just one afternoon? That you could find key market gaps and identify consumer language most likely to motivate purchase without spending a dime?

Well, if you've got an internet connection and a few hours to spare, it's absolutely true! *(Even if you don't have an existing list of prospects and customers, you can still get 80 percent of the benefit one afternoon.)*

How do I know? Because I'm the guy who used to bill companies like Bausch & Lomb, Whirlpool, and Nabisco $100,000 to $500,000 per project for time-tested, proven marketing research systems that virtually eliminate risk, guesswork, and uncertainty.

In fact, my wife and I have billed over 20 million dollars for these kinds of projects—and counting. I've also built and sold an internet advertising agency, developed several of my own highly profitable internet businesses, and maintain a nice practice of high-end internet consulting clients.

If you'll forgive my immodesty for a moment *(and promise not to tell my mom about my bragging)* I'm probably THE guy who's thought longer and harder about online market intelligence than anyone else in the world. So I hope you'll listen to me when I tell you we're at a unique turning point in history, a time when HUGE insights into ANY market can be gathered online by the savvy entrepreneur who knows where to look!

Here's a summary of what you'll learn if you pay close attention to the next few pages. If it hasn't hit you yet here's a newsflash: The internet is organized by keyword! And if you put some thought into selecting your bull's-eye keyword (the single most important keyword in your market):

- You can pull consumer language from social media around your keyword, and organize it in a FREE newsreader program (Twitter, YouTube, high-profile blogs, forums, newsgroups, Google Alerts, etc.).
- You can survey prospects and customers in your market (either from your own existing lists or from social media gathering places) to find out what their most pressing needs are.
- You can apply a special scoring method to identify who the most HYPER-RESPONSIVE prospects and customers are in these systems, then cater your advertising to match their needs.

In short, there's no need for you to continue playing what Dan Kennedy calls "blind archery!" Why guess when you can know?

Let's look at each of these simple techniques in more detail.

The "Bull's-Eye" Social Media Technique

If you could advertise on only ONE keyword phrase online, what would that keyword be? If you had to describe your business using only ONE search phrase, what would it be?

This might be the single most important question you'll ever answer about your business, because once you do, you can easily narrow your field of competitors and focus on the exact "corner of the internet" you'd like to dominate. (You can't become "king of the mountain" until you identify what mountain you'd like to climb.)

Most of my clients hesitate to complete this exercise for fear of reducing their profit volume. But as a practical matter, I find exactly the opposite is true—*as long as you select a keyword with sufficient volume and one that other advertisers are paying money to be seen on*—because selecting your most important keyword FORCES you to create a strong position/brand in the market, which in turn becomes a kind of "center of gravity" that pulls in people from way beyond your initial keyword focus.

For my "mathematical proof" of this point, download the free ebook at http://www.glennlivingston.com/AM.php.

Google has a keyword tool that is essential to any market research project. Just go to Google and search "Google keyword tool," and it'll be the first thing that comes up. It tells you how many people search for anything you type in. For example, if I type in "guinea pigs," Google shows me this, in Figure 21–1.

Keyword	Competition	Global Monthly Searches [?]	Local Monthly Searches [?]
where to find **guinea pigs** ▾	Low	1,000,000	450,000
what are **guinea pigs** ▾	Low	1,000,000	450,000
where to get **guinea pigs** ▾	Low	1,000,000	450,000
where are **guinea pigs** from ▾	Low	1,000,000	450,000
about **guinea pigs** ▾	Low	1,000,000	450,000
guinea pigs on sale ▾	Medium	49,500	22,200
guinea pigs for sale ▾	Medium	49,500	22,200
guinea pigs sale ▾	Medium	49,500	22,200
cages for **guinea pigs** ▾	High	49,500	27,100
guinea pigs cages ▾	High	49,500	27,100
guinea pigs cage ▾	High	49,500	27,100
cage for **guinea pigs** ▾	High	49,500	27,100
guinea pigs eat ▾	Low	40,500	22,200
what **guinea pigs** eat ▾	Low	40,500	22,200

Figure 21–1. Google keyword tool results for "guinea pigs."

The tool reports bid prices, search volumes by country, and related keywords. This is a whole subject in and of itself, and Perry explores it more in his book *Ultimate Guide to Google AdWords* and in his free course at www.perrymarshall.com/google/.

Once you know your single most important keyword, follow this simple, step-by-step procedure:

- Go to www.TweetGrid.com and set up a 1 x 1 marquee for it. (Free.) Periodically browse the conversations passing by on this keyword,

and just copy and paste any tweets which strike you as a) representing significant frustration in the market; b) expressing direct
benefits of a product or service, especially in an emotional way; or
c) suggestive of a WISH the prospect or customer might have.

- Be sure to ignore advertiser tweets, as you're only looking for the
prospects/customers. Gather all these tweets in a document. (Note:
This is not a quantitative exercise but more of a substitute for
attending a trade conference or fan club meeting where you can get
an immersion experience with your market.)

- Go to YouTube, then search and watch any videos, looking for the
same kinds of things. Take notes in a separate document.

- Go to http://Blogsearch.Google.com and www.Technorati.com,
and find the highest-profile blogs for your keyword. Read the articles, and especially look for comments. Keep notes in your document.

- Go to www.google.com/alerts and set up alerts on the keyword
(one for news, one for web, etc.). Keep notes in your document.

Gather all the relevant language you can from all of the above,
then go through and highlight the 20 percent of tweets, video text, blog
comments, and alert text which seems longest, most engaged, and/or
most passionate. This provides your *first clue* regarding market gaps and
what the most responsive customers are likely to desire because hyper-
responsive customers are MUCH more likely to engage in social media
as such.

What patterns to you notice? Anything missing in the market? Is there
a contrarian position that might be suggested by the data? Something that
says that a marketer like you should get up on the roof and shout "No!
You're not being taken care of by the other vendors in this market, and it's
absolutely outrageous! Why isn't anyone talking about this?" (For a much
more in-depth look at how this works, please see www.glennlivingston.
com/AD.php.)

- What you're looking for is that one critical need that might dis-
tinguish YOU as different and better than every other competitor
vying for attention on your bull's-eye keyword. I call this a "point of

difference" benefit, and it's THE critical component of a successful marketing strategy.

- "Point of Difference" benefits are what make people likely to choose YOU to give money to, as compared to "price of entry" benefits which are the things EVERY vendor has to deliver just to be "in the running" for the purchase.

- For example, I used to sell a set of educational CDs that taught people how to profitably raise alpacas. Alpacas are a unique animal that costs between $5,000 to $15,000 each AND were associated with lucrative tax advantages, so this education was very valuable. But everyone else in the market was just telling the prospect the basics: how to get started without any money, how to feed them, how much land is needed.

- My research suggested potential buyers really wanted the DETAILS of the tax implications, and they wanted to hear them from experts. So I stood up and said things like, "Be careful! Don't set up an alpaca business until you hear these detailed interviews with Certified Public Accountants who specialize in alpaca farming businesses! Why isn't anyone else providing this for you?"

- As you can imagine, it was very effective.

- In addition to these key "Point of Difference" benefits, you're also looking for examples of specific "page of customer's diary" language you can echo back to make the sale. For example, if you were selling desktop computers and you found that hyper-responsives on your target keyword were saying things like "I want a computer that just frickin' boots up quickly so I can get on with my work!" you could echo back near the top of your landing page, "Some of the World's Fastest-Booting Computers: So You Can Get on with Your Work!" (See where I'm going with this?) Continuing in our quest for hyper-responsive points of different and key consumer language, let's move to the . . .

80/20 Survey Technique for Hyper-Responsive Intelligence

Ninety-nine percent of marketers have absolutely NO idea how to use surveys. They think they're supposed to ask people what their most important question or need is, then just echo these needs back to them in priority order, kind of like a FAQ. But the problem with Frequently **Asked** Questions is that they're also Frequently **Answered** Questions. Frequently Presented Needs are also Frequently Catered To Needs

In other words, all a standard survey does for you is identify the price of entry benefits for a market. It doesn't give you any way of distinguishing what needs represent the market gap or where you might position yourself with POINT OF DIFFERENCE benefits.

Moreover, these surveys typically don't ask WHY the respondent is experiencing the frustration they're experiencing, which really castrates the purpose of doing the survey in the first place.

For example, it's infinitely more powerful to know that 40 percent of your prospects need a computer that boots up quickly *because* they're paid based upon per-unit productivity, for example, than just knowing they need a fast boot. In the former case, you don't know how to paint the mood and tone of your advertising, whereas in the latter you know it's all about the frustrations of per-unit workers.

Here's a simple way to fix this problem. Ask them not only WHAT their single most important question or need is relating to your topic, but WHY they chose to look for a solution today and HOW DIFFICULT it was to find a good one. Then score it using the protocol in the next section (which also takes into account the level of engagement of each prospect).

Pareto Point

The 80/20 Protocol

Send these three questions to your prospect and customer list (or recruit people via forums, Twitter, Facebook, and other social media gathering places on your bull's-eye keyword):

- The WHAT question: "What's your single most important question about ___? (Keyword)"
- The WHY question: "Why would it make a difference in your life to get a good answer for this problem or find a solution for your need? (Details, please.)"
- The HOW DIFFICULT question: "How difficult has it been for you to find a good answer for the above to date?" (Not at all difficult, somewhat difficult, very difficult.)

So what do you do with this information?

Quick and dirty summary: You throw it into a spreadsheet. You discard the "not difficult" and "somewhat difficult" and you keep only the "very difficult." Those are the people who really have an itch that they can't figure out how to scratch.

Then you throw away the short answers and keep the long answers. What's left are your highly influential 5 to 10 percent who will actually give you money for a product that solves their problems. Their answers are literally a page out of their diary. And you'll know exactly what problems your product has to solve.

There's a much better approach, however, one that's much more precise. I have devised a simple scoring system for your survey, and you can download it at www.perrymarshall.com/8020supplement.

When you're done, sort your data by this score ("hyper-responsive score"), and look at the top 20 percent of responses. Or if you have thousands of responses, look at the top 5 percent instead. THESE are your most hyper-responsive prospects, and it's within those responses you'll find the most motivating language, needs and your point of difference benefit.

To listen to a full-length interview where Perry Marshall and I discuss depth-research techniques you can leverage in the modern internet era, please visit www.LivingstonReport.com.

PARETO SUMMARY

▷ It pays to answer a question in a marketplace only if it's a question that nobody else is answering.

▷ You can find the questions people ask and the exact language they ask them in with social media. Social media is for listening more than it's for talking.

▷ Google's keyword tool tells you how many people are searching for solutions.

▷ When you solve the most urgent problems that the most responsive 5 percent are searching for, you hit pay dirt.

1,000 Things to Pay Attention to—Only Three or Four Matter Right Now

Ten years ago if you actually did the testing and tracking that I teach today, you might be considered an advertising astrophysicist. Today, disciplined testing is *absolutely necessary* if you want to dominate a market online.

Nowadays most people still don't do it, truth be told, and don't make much progress. This is truly what separates the winners from the losers. Almost all of the dozens of entrepreneurs who I coached to do this in the past year have made massive progress: double-digit growth, sometimes even doubling or tripling in just a few months.

The short list of things to test and track are:

- Money In, Money Out
- Click-Thru Rates of Google ads
- Conversions of specific keywords to sales

Pareto
Point

- Opt-in and lead-generation pages
- Sales pages and order forms
- Individual traffic sources (affiliates, banner ads, email promotions)

The problem most people have with this is they quickly get overwhelmed with details and data. You end up drowning in a sea of numbers, and you're still not sure why you're not making more money.

Let's break this down and make it really simple.

First, let's understand that most important of all is: **Dollars in/dollars out.** Now, maybe it should seem unnecessary to say this, but I've had consultations with people who had no idea what their numbers actually are. I had one student who, as far as I could tell, seemed to be making pretty good money but was extremely frustrated with her progress. Since she didn't know dollars in/dollars out, there was no benchmark with which to judge.

No web tracking system I've ever seen gives perfectly accurate numbers. But dollars in the bank—that's a pretty reliable measure.

Figure 22–1 shows Square One.

Square Two looks like Figure 22–2.

Figure 22–1. Square One.

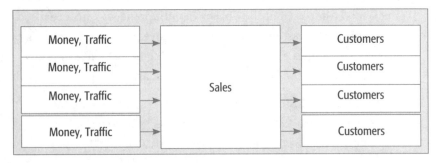

Figure 22–2. Square Two.

The first step is figuring out where the good prospects are and where they aren't. These could come from mailing lists, email lists, keywords, other peoples' web pages, print ads, postcards, Facebook ads, banner ads, affiliates, joint venture partners. The most important factor is the type of people you're marketing to.

The next step is breaking your sales funnel into pieces. If your sales process doesn't work, break it up into pieces and make the pieces work. Step 1 might be an opt-in. Step 2 might be a phone conversation or a teleseminar. Step 3 might be the sale.

"Money, Traffic, and Prospects A" might get 15 percent opt-ins and "Money, Traffic, and Prospects B" also get 15 percent opt-ins. But Source A gets you no buyers, and Source B brings a lot of buyers. This is very common!

The astute reader will recognize that if we're really keeping our eye on the ball, we've got 12 things to measure now, not four. Four traffic sources and three steps for each one. The parts of the sales funnel you watch now look like Figure 22–3.

Figure 22–3. Regardless of what happens in the middle, you need to know how many people and how many dollars are going in and out of your sales funnel.

If you're doing Pay-Per-Click, you don't have four traffic sources—you might 400 or 4,000. Multiply that by two, three, four steps in the sales process and maybe a few dozen products—how are you ever going to track that?

Answer: You don't.

What to Measure, What to Track, What to Ignore

Let's say you've got 12 keywords you're tracking and you've got 12 different actions you want people to take. In this example the 12 different actions are:

- A $100 product, a $250 product, a $500 product, and a $1000 product (four product choices)
- Opt-in, telephone conversation, receive product trial sample (three steps in the sales funnel)

If you want to connect all the dots, you've got 144 things to measure. If you put all 144 combinations on a spreadsheet, it would look like this:

1	2	3	4	5	6	7	8	9	10	11	12
13	14	15	16	17	18	19	20	21	22	23	24
25	26	27	28	29	30	31	32	33	34	35	36
37	38	39	40	41	42	43	44	45	46	47	48
49	50	51	52	53	54	55	56	57	58	59	60
61	62	63	64	65	66	67	68	69	70	71	72
73	74	75	76	77	78	79	80	81	82	83	84
85	86	87	88	89	90	91	92	93	94	95	96
97	98	99	100	101	102	103	104	105	106	107	108
109	110	111	112	113	114	115	116	117	118	119	120
121	122	123	124	125	126	127	128	129	130	131	132
133	134	135	136	137	138	139	140	141	142	143	144

Figure 22–4. If you pretend everything's equal, all the ingredients in your sales funnel look like this.

There are several problems with this: It's too much data to reasonably keep track of, and perhaps the least obvious problem is that box Number 142 may turn an insanely high ROI this week (from ONE customer who bought ONE time) and box Number 43 gives you a big fat zero. You eliminate Number 143 but what you don't know is that Number 142 was pure luck—it never happens again—and Number 143 would have performed nicely if you'd given it more time.

The problem here is we drew this thing the wrong way. All the squares are the same size! What we ignored is 80/20—the fact that cause and effect are ALWAYS disproportionate. The grid gets drawn much differently if we understand that *every dimension of your sales machine has a disproportionate relationship between cause and effect.*

We had 12 keywords, right?

Three or four of them are going to bring most of the traffic. In fact, if you've got 2,000 keywords, 95 percent of your traffic is probably going to come from fewer than 20 of them. Do you need to track the other 1980 keywords?

Well, you're sure not going to spend hours and hours setting up elaborate tracking for each one!

We had four products—and one or two of them is going to produce most of the sales. We had three steps in the sales funnel; let's say the opt-in is a prerequisite for all sales, so the other two steps are the ones that actually flip the buyers. So what do we have on our shortlist?

- Three keywords
- Two products
- Two sales funnel steps
- 3 x 2 x 2 = 12

Now we're down to just 12 things to watch, not 144. Three keywords, two products, two steps. That's manageable!

Here's the RIGHT way to draw the grid—the 80/20 Sales Matrix (see Figure 22–5 on page 176).

The columns represent keywords. Three of them bring more than half the traffic.

The rows represent combinations of products and sales steps. The top three combinations, like the keywords, also bring more than half the traffic.

If you pay attention to *only* 1, 2, 13, and 14 in your matrix, you're covering more than a third of your business with only four things to think about. If you pay attention to *only* 1, 2, 3, 4, 13, 14, 15, 16, 25, 26, 27, and 28, you're covering more than half your business with only 12 things to think about.

And if you focus your attention on making the big squares bigger—doubling them, let's say—then you grow your business 50 percent with one-tenth the effort.

Let's say it takes you a week of work to double a square. Do you want to double square Number 1 or square Number 77? In four weeks you can double some little squares, or double some big squares.

It's up to you.

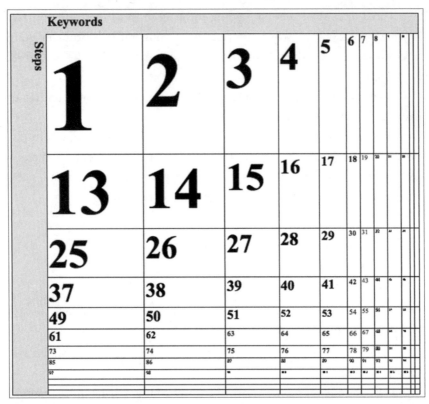

Figure 22–5. This is what cause and effect really look like, for all the ways that you touch a customer in order to influence a sale.

What Matters Most in Your Matrix?

Obviously it's the *big* squares that deserve the attention. For square number one and the other big squares, you need to measure *everything.* Know your numbers to the penny. So here's an example, from Julie Brumlik's Google campaign for Dremu Skincare. See Figure 22–6 on page 177.

This particular campaign is organized very well: two ads rotating, and a very narrow band of closely related keywords (and no other keywords) in this group; she's tracking sales conversions and adjusting bids on each keyword accordingly.

Notice how this group is sorted: by **clicks.** The keyword with the most clicks is "skin care" with 4,216 clicks. Out of 7,576 total clicks, that's 56 percent of all the clicks just from *one* keyword. More than 80 percent of the traffic comes from the top *three* keywords.

| Tools: ▸Filter Keywords \| ▸Add Keywords \| Edit Keywords \| Keyword Tool - New! | | | | | | | 1 - 19 of 19 keywords. | | | |

As seen on Oprah	◆ Create New Ad: Text Ad | Image Ad	◉ this month ▾
The skin care products celebrities use before they put on makeup. www.dremu.com	1 of 2 Ads: View all below	○ Dec ▾ 1 ▾ 2005 ▾ - Dec ▾ 15 ▾ 2005 ▾ Go
Delete Edit CPCs/URLs		☐ Include deleted items that were active in this date range

☐ Keyword	Status [?]	Current Bid Max CPC	Clicks ▼	Impr.	CTR	Avg. CPC	Cost	Avg. Pos	Conv. Rate	Cost/Conv.
Search Total	Enabled	Default $0.15 [edit]	7,576	301,173	2.5%	$0.31	$2,296.96	4.2	1.00%	$30.22
Content Total [?]	Not enabled		0	0	-	-	-	-	0.00%	$0.00
☐ "skin care"	Active	$0.45	4,216	136,262	3.0%	$0.33	$1,383.37	3.7	1.19%	$27.67
☐ skin products	Active	$0.35	1,071	40,159	2.6%	$0.26	$278.38	4.4	0.75%	$34.80
☐ skin cream	Active	$0.35	923	32,937	2.8%	$0.28	$258.00	4.6	0.54%	$51.60
☐ skin care	Active	$0.45	391	19,369	2.0%	$0.33	$127.03	3.5	1.28%	$25.41
☐ [skin care]	Active	$0.35	249	28,734	0.8%	$0.31	$76.01	5.8	0.40%	$76.01
☐ [skin care products]	Active	$0.30	179	4,259	4.2%	$0.28	$48.86	3.2	0.00%	$0.00
☐ "skincare"	Active	$0.25	138	4,726	2.9%	$0.21	$28.45	5.8	1.45%	$14.23
☐ "skin care products"	Active	$0.35	109	19,722	0.5%	$0.30	$32.39	3.8	0.92%	$32.39

Figure 22–6. Clicks in a Google ad campaign, sorted by keyword from most-clicked to least.

These top three keywords matter a lot. The keywords with fewer than 100 clicks hardly matter at all. The next step in developing this is to peel-and-stick the top two to three words and put each in its own group, all by itself. The keyword "skin care" gets enough traffic, all by itself, to merit tracking sales conversion on each individual ad.

CTR is important, but which ad gets the most buyers? Most people never bother with this—it's admittedly pretty granular. But for one keyword that costs $2,500 a month, it's worth tracking those fine details. Google will tell you sales conversion rates for individual ads.

This one keyword may deserve its own special landing page, which should also be tracked. Yep, that's more details to look after. But it means you can mostly ignore the fine details on hundreds of other keywords.

At any given time, there are only three to four things you need to focus on to get your business to the next level. Three to four keywords in your present Google campaign. Three to four pages on your website. A couple of critical steps in your sales funnel. A couple of products. One or two critical salespeople.

Pareto Point

It's not that the other stuff doesn't matter, because it does. But it deserves the *minority* of your attention. Your job is to figure out what the main thing is and keep the main thing the main thing. You don't "peel and stick" the six-word keyword phrase that gets 15 impressions a month; it would take four years to get meaningful numbers anyway.

"OK, So If I've Tweaked E-V-E-R-Y-T-H-I-N-G to the Max That's Inside One of the Big Squares, What Do I Do Now?"

Next: Look for the Next Big Thing. I don't know what that is for you, but it's likely to be something from the following list:

1. A super-deluxe version of your product at four times the price.
2. An unmet need that nobody in your market is dealing with, and pent-up demand.
3. If you perform a service, sell a product that teaches 'em how to do it. If you sell a how-to product, perform the service.
4. If you sell a service, add a physical product. If you sell a physical product, add a service.
5. If you've tapped out your existing market, take your skills into a new market.
6. Repackage your product or combine it with other products to create more dimensions of value.
7. If you sell something on a one-time basis, turn it into repeat purchases with a membership.

Marketers have so many e-books, have listened to so many teleseminars, have heard so many "great ideas" that they're just overloaded. They have *way too many options*. My job in many cases is to eliminate options, and narrow things down to the three to four actions that will get them the most bang for the buck.

PARETO SUMMARY

▷ Any time you have a complex business with lots of moving parts, you can make a simple matrix that shows you which small hinges swing big doors.

▷ You can optimize half of your process by optimizing the most important 5 percent.

▷ Once you've optimized **T**raffic and **C**onversion, turn your focus back to Economics.

CHAPTER

23

RFM: The 3-D 80/20 of Profitable Marketing

Pareto Point

RFM is about who you pay attention to in your business, based on who's paying attention to you. It's a feedback loop, in the same way the testing/tracking sales improvement process is a feedback loop. You pour more and more energy into the stuff that's already working, less and less into what you have clearly determined is not working.

RFM Is

- **Recency**. How recently has your customer purchased? Which customers have bought something, say, in the last 90 days?
- **Frequency**. How often has your customer purchased? Which customers have repeatedly bought things from you?

- **Money**. How much has your customer spent? Which customers have spent the most with you?

Large, corporate direct marketers—established catalog and mail order companies, frequent-flier programs, companies who spend large sums of money selling to lists of people—know this stuff cold. (That's why the credit card companies manage to successfully acquire customers even though the copy in their letters stinks—because they know exactly who to send their lousy letters to, and when.)

At DM industry trade shows I've met consultants who perform exotic data analysis on huge databases. In their world, RFM is "database kindergarten." This is so basic, it's standard practice in mailing lists to have a "90-day hotline" list of buyers you can rent, for an additional fee. But again, most entrepreneurs and online marketers are totally unaware of this.

Also be warned: Unscrupulous list brokers will sell you the 90-day list when you're testing but not tell you, giving you an over-optimistic impression of how good their list is. Caveat emptor. (See Chapter 6 for more detailed discussion of lists.)

RFM is a matrix, too—each customer represents a *combination* of R, F, and M—and once again you can focus your limited resources on a relatively small fraction of your customers and get hugely disproportionate returns.

Remember the 80/20 sales process matrix I showed you? **Here's the same thing for RFM, except that it's 3-D and not 2-D.**

In Figure 23–1, page 181, each little cube inside the big cube represents one customer. Notice the great big customer on the top-front corner—don't you think he deserves some special attention?

How do you go from 2-D to 3-D? It's easy. You rank customers from most recent to least recent; you rank them from most frequent to least frequent and most money to least money. You can do all of this in a single spreadsheet with columns that score them on a scale from 1–10 for R, F, and M. Then you say, "I only want customers whose R+F+M score is greater than 20."

The size of each cube in the matrix represents the merit of spending money to market to that customer. If you can form even a crude picture

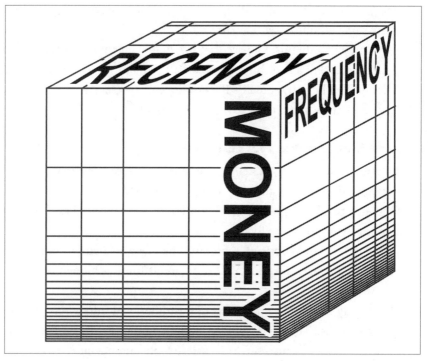

Figure 23-1. Recency, Frequency, and Money all obey 80/20. The three combined together focus huge profits in a very small number of squares.

of your business from this perspective, you have in your possession a most valuable tool.

The way I've drawn Figure 23-1, there's maybe 400 customers or so. Notice that the majority of them have spent relatively little money, seldom returned, and haven't bought anything for quite some time.

It's one thing to hear about this or see it on a spreadsheet, it's another thing to see it visually. This is the 80/20 rule the way it *really* works in the real world—in not one, but three, four, and five dimensions.

Multiplied out, it's really 95/5 or 99/1. One percent of what you own and do produces 99 percent of the results. Keep this picture in your mind. Incorporate this into your picture of marketing, advertising, and customer retention—it will inform many if not most decisions and save you LOTS of effort.

Obviously if you're going to send out direct mail or do any kind of marketing that costs money, this is a great way to carve the junk out of the list and cut your costs by a third or half or two-thirds, since every envelope costs the same amount of money to send.

And if you study this, you see that out of 400 customers, a few dozen customers represent a kick-butt return on investment. You don't just send 'em a letter. Maybe you send a FedEx envelope or special package. A gift at Christmas. A wine and cheese party, a VIP reception.

Have an Expert Analyze Your Customers

Kristalytics (www.kristalytics.com) has a very interesting service. Send them your customer list, and they will give you extremely detailed demographic and psychographic information about your customers. This can tremendously improve the focus of your advertising targets.

Similarly, Brian Woodruff, who built the www.8020curve.com site, is a data-mining expert. Data mining is all about finding hidden 80/20s in your customer list.

It's highly likely that most of your customers fall into a very narrow range of profiles. They live only in certain kinds of places; they have only certain ranges of income. Most salespeople and business owners are already vaguely aware of this, but have never given it a serious look.

If you are selling to an existing customer list, you can greatly enhance your efforts by sending direct mail, calling them on the phone, etc. But a portion of those past customers will be very responsive, and large numbers of them will not be, and that costs you money. It's possible to predict with surprising accuracy who will buy again and who won't. Kristalytics can often cut waste by 50 percent or more by telling you who on your list is most likely to respond.

Does RFM Matter if Email Is Free Anyway?

Yessiree Bob. I'd go as far as to say the greatest mistake email marketers make is assuming it doesn't.

Here's why you should pay close attention to this: Let's say you've got 10,000 people on your email list: 9,000 of them are non-buyers, and 1,000 of them are buyers. Five hundred have bought twice or recently and 100 of them buy pretty much everything you sell and have even bought really expensive upgrades.

In other words, the Power Curve shows peoples' level of interest in your email list. The bottom 10 percent don't want to hear from you ever again. The top 1 percent would like to hear from you at least once a day. Maybe twice.

Let's say you're just about to announce a super-elite advanced model that costs twice as much as anything else you've ever offered. Should you send it out to the whole list? You *may* sell the most by sending it to the whole list; after all, even from a big list of non-buyers you'll usually find one or two who will make the big leap.

But fact is, the vast majority of your sales will come from the top 500 people on your list. And the fact is, your offer is of no interest whatsoever to almost everyone in the bottom 9,000, the non-buyers. It may just irritate them. A 0.01 percent response may *seem* acceptable ROI for an email list, but there's a cost: the irritation factor. *You might get two buyers, but you taught most of the other 8,998 that they should ignore your emails.* (Especially if your email was all sales pitch and no content.)

There's another benefit to sending small email blasts instead of big ones: They're much more likely to get delivered. The large ISPs like Yahoo, Hotmail, and AOL let single email messages through unimpeded.

But as soon as they get hit with a significant number, the emails automatically go into the "wait and see" bucket. Then the email goes through the spam filters, where you may be on the gray list or blacklist. A small blast to 100 to 200 is comparatively safe from spam filters.

Segment Your Email Lists

Most people take advantage of the "free" delivery of email the wrong way: send it just because it's free. The *right* way is to build sublists. If you've got 10,000 people total on your list, you ought to have those people segmented into at least a half-dozen or dozen categories according to what products and services and information topics they're interested in.

Now your job is to come up with offers and content that match those peoples' wants, needs, and desires. That's what makes your list responsive.

You segment email lists any number of ways, depending on the sophistication of your email program. I use InfusionSoft, which allows you to "tag" people who bought a certain product, opened a certain email, clicked on a link, filled out a form. Any of those activities can add a person to a list, and it puts people on multiple lists. Some might be only on one "sublist," and others might be on a hundred. And it doesn't just add up, it multiplies.

You've just discovered how to take dozens of traffic sources, hundreds of keywords, dozens of paths through your website, hundreds of web pages and thousands of prospects and customers—and focus modest amounts of effort on very small pieces of the puzzle—and get huge returns, far out of proportion to what you put in. *Leverage.*

If you haven't gotten at least $10,000 of value from this chapter, you ain't tryin', baby! Here's to *massive leverage* for you in the 21st century.

PARETO SUMMARY

▷ The 80/20 of valuable customers is: Recency, Frequency, Money.

▷ You measure: customers in, dollars in, sales out, dollars out.

▷ You can find thousands of things to measure, test, and optimize, but at any given time, only three to four really matter.

▷ You can grow your business 50 percent by optimizing the most important 1 percent.

"My Latte's Too Foamy!"

My fave rave professor from college, Dr. Robert Knoll, pointed his bony finger at us freshmen, early first semester. He pronounced: "Half your battles were won for you before you were even born, and don't you forget it."

I got my first taste of Dr. Knoll's great truth in São Paulo, Brazil.

In Chicago, you'll find the occasional homeless person living under a bridge. But São Paulo manages to fit an entire suburb under the same bridge. (A politician might win an election just by swinging the "bridge people" vote.)

When you stretch a rubber band, it never goes back to its original size. My brain cells creaked and groaned for weeks, absorbing that experience. New cultures hugely expand your mind. They change you at a cellular level.

There in Brazil, Laura and I determined that if finances ever permitted, we'd make such visits a habit, so we would never forget how the other half lives.

For the last decade we've made that our practice.

Cuyler ("Number-One Son") was 5 months old when we went to Brazil; now he's 14. His older sister Tannah is 16. They live a nice cushy American life in Chicago. Occasionally they exhibit signs of entitlement, and we hear them say stuff like, "My latte's too foamy!"

(To produce the proper effect, read the above sentence aloud in a petulant, whiny voice.)

This could only mean one thing:

They're old enough. Time to take 'em to the jagged edge.

Laura's brother Alan runs a relief agency, ChildrensRelief.org. The Jagged Edge IS Alan's Unique Selling Proposition.

Alan says, "Come to Calcutta. You won't be disappointed. I'll hook you up with Smriti."

In America, Calcutta is as famous for Mother Theresa's work as anything else. Alan's got his own mini-version of Mother Theresa, Smriti. Her turf is the Red Light district. She trains ex-prostitutes how to sew, offering them marketplace skills and an escape from the sex trade. She also runs a school that teaches their children how to read and write.

Tannah's studying French in school, so we stopped in Paris on the way to India. We admired steel towers and Gothic buildings and dined on crêpes for a couple days.

Then, 20 hours of airplanes and airports later, we found ourselves in India's grittiest city.

If you enjoy driving on the left side of the street in a 40-year-old yellow taxi where the driver shuts the engine off at every stoplight, horns blare nonstop, where rickety buses crammed with passengers spew soot into your window . . . if you enjoy a city where guys urinate on the side of the road and insistent beggars march into the street in gridlocked traffic and split test every passenger and car window . . . you'll love Calcutta.

Calcutta does not disappoint. It's monsoon season. Ninety-five percent humidity, sweltering. My glasses steamed up every time we went outside.

My driver picked us up from the airport late in the afternoon. As we dodged bicycles, donkey carts, and rickshaws he explained the trolleys: Regular fare is four rupees (two cents), and the deluxe fare is five rupees (two and a half cents).

The difference? The deluxe-fare trolley has a ceiling fan.

The first place Smriti took us was to the Kalighat temple, home of Kali, the Hindu goddess of destruction, who is always depicted with a decapitated head in one hand. Calcutta is named in her honor.

We headed up the street into the Red Light district, a bazaar of dingy buildings, pock-marked pavement, milling crowds, and vendor stalls. Smriti took Tannah's hand, and I walked with Cuyler. Every block or so, Smriti would bump into someone she knew, usually a prostitute.

This being a different culture, it was not immediately obvious to me which women were "on duty." I knew for safety's sake that Smriti was sidestepping the seedier boulevards. She vaguely alluded to what we were avoiding by not going there.

We met a lovely, slender girl with sharp features. She looked about Cuyler's age. We greeted her, and she and Smriti spoke for a bit. Smriti said, "She's recently married." *The girl seemed awfully young for that.* As we walked on and later had dinner, she explained to Tannah what that actually meant.

"These women come from Bangladesh or West Bengal. They come to here and join the sex trade because of their poverty. While they're entertaining clients in the night, their kids go out and get food and supply their moms with whatever else they need to support the business.

"That 13-year-old married girl you met—her husband is 20 to 30 years older than she is. They marry young to much older men because they've got zero money and the man's got cash."

Oh, I see . . . he's her *sugar daddy.*

Smriti adds: "As these women stay involved in this work, they become very cold and hardened."

We finish eating, buy a gift for Laura back at home and return to our hotel.

Tannah says to me, "Hey, remember that 'Half your battles were won for you before you were ever born' thing?"

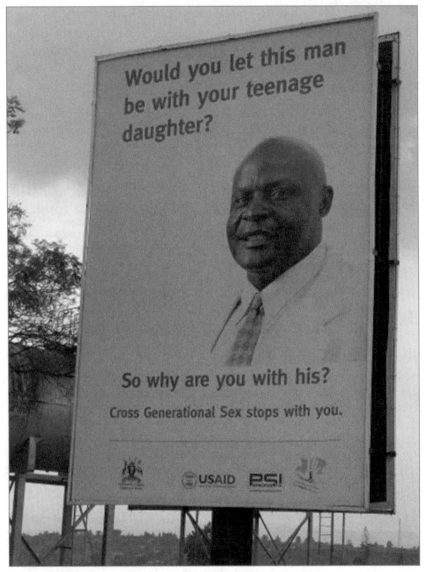

Figure 24–1. The edgiest ad I've ever seen: Taking on the "sugar daddy" phenomenon in Uganda. (Photo courtesy Matt Kehn.)

"Yeah."

"Dad, I GET it. Can we go home now?"

Half those girls' battles were LOST for them before they were ever born. That, along with the chaos and screeching horns and grime and dingy flats—kinda makes the stairs in the Paris Metro station that reeked of urine seem a lot less dreadful.

She Facebooks her friends at home: "If you thought the subway in Paris was filthy, you should try Calcutta."

That's what life is like for the bottom 20 percent.

Every debate about capitalism vs. socialism vs. communism, every election debate, is really a battle over 80/20.

If you put 1,000 people in a room, the difference between the most financially able person and the least is at least 400:1. Considering some folks might be mentally handicapped and some might be 6 months old and wearing diapers, the inequalities are astronomical.

By now, you know that 80/20 truly is a law of nature and there is nothing anyone can do to change it. Everyone struggles with the question: "How do we deal with the extreme inequality in the world?"

Fact: There are some people who, no matter how hard they try, will not be able to "make it" in the hard realities that inevitably flow from the 80/20 principle.

Fact: There are some people who, without seeming to even try all that hard, make more money than they can possibly spend. 80/20 sees to it that money keeps flowing their way.

You can't legislate 80/20 away, you can't tax it away, you can't educate it away, you can't wish it away.

So how do you work with it? What do you do?

I've spent the last 10 years thinking about this. Here are some truths I've arrived at:

You cannot fix this problem from the *outside*, because in the end, 80/20 still always wins. You can only fix it from the inside.

The catastrophe of communism illustrates this. Did communism solve 80/20? No, it actually made it worse, because there was still a small minority of people who made a thousand times as much money as everyone else. Workers pretended to work, and the party pretended to pay them.

The progressive tax schedules of Western countries partly solve the problem by taxing the rich at higher rates than the poor, but countries undoubtedly pay a price for this.

I talked to a friend who referred to himself as a "tax exile." He used to live in the United Kingdom, but he moved all his assets to an island whose income tax form takes up one side of one piece of paper. The U.K. has now lost this gentleman's estate and his entire company. I talked to another from the United States just this week who is seriously considering moving to Costa Rica.

And even if people don't physically move to other countries, the wealthiest people *always* find ways to keep their money out of the government's hands. If not all, at least the smart ones.

Interestingly, I talked to another person, also this week, who had made millions of dollars, reached retirement age, sold his huge house, moved into a modest place, and gave most of what he owned to charity.

Pareto
Point

Charity Is Turning 80/20 Upside Down. That's an Inside Job.

Every millionaire, every billionaire, can freely decide to give of his wealth. That same person, unencumbered by taxes and guided by conscience, can invest his money in growing companies and countries and economies. When he puts his mind to it, he can enormously propel the activity and the future of everyone around him.

When you tax that person, all you accomplish is moving money from capable, enterprising hands to wasteful, bureaucratic hands.

Government most certainly has its place, but any politician who tells you he can solve inequality through policy alone is either lying or deluded.

Charity and the will to do good can come only from the heart. And it does good *for* your heart. It enriches your life.

When an economy is blessed with good-hearted wealthy people who sincerely wish to make the world a better place, it will prosper. When the wealthiest people are greedy and corrupt and self-centered, no amount of legislation will ever fix it.

Pure 80/20 Is Depressingly Darwinian, Especially When You're on the Bottom.

This book began with a guy racking a shotgun and ended up just down the street from Mother Theresa's apartment. There's a reason why. You need to be careful not to take 80/20 too far.

80/20 is why 20 percent of the people in the world live on less than a dollar a day. And if people don't have the **will** to change that, it's not going to change.

Voting to raise other peoples' taxes is not an act of generosity. **Generosity starts with you. Not "them."** And it starts now, not someday when you're rich and successful. Compared to many, you're rich and successful now.

My personal experience is that giving has this funny way of coming back to you. I can't tell you how many people from all kinds of different walks of life and religions and worldviews have said, "You can't out-give God."

The cold hard facts of 80/20 are the reason why generosity is the *only* thing that will sustain the weakest and most disadvantaged. Pure 80/20 thinking can only reinforce the status quo. In Charles Dickens' *A Christmas Carol,* Ebenezer Scrooge ruthlessly practices 80/20. It takes a terrifying vision of the future to jolt him out of the ruthlessly pragmatic, 80/20 bubble he's been living in.

This is why religious traditions insist that you should take a percentage of your money right off the top and give it to the poor. When everyone gives their 10 percent—especially the people at the top of the heap—*there's always enough money to take care of the people at the bottom of the heap.*

That 10 percent is very powerful, by the way, and a dollar also stretches farther at the bottom than at the top. I speak from experience. Every time you give, you make a statement of personal power and autonomy: "I am not a slave to money. Money is my slave. I believe I will always have enough, and more is coming my way."

An awful lot of us have done time on the bottom of some heap, somewhere. It's not a fun place to be. So while most entrepreneurs and salespeople are ignorant about 80/20, it's a mistake to be too mercenary about it. You can alienate a lot of people real fast. The legendary marketer Jeff Paul said, "Be nice to people on your way up, because you meet the very same people on the way down."

This also means that you must be mindful about how you deal with the top and bottom 20 percent. The generous 80/20 entrepreneur focuses on the top 20 percent of his customer base, giving maximum value and extracting maximum profit. That's why he has enough money to build a school for AIDS orphans in Nairobi, who live on the bottom of the spectrum.

If he invested all his generosity on "average Americans" or low-value customers, or charged too little for his services and helped clients who couldn't afford his fees, he wouldn't have anything left for the weakest of the weak who really need the help.

Inequality vs. Equality

By 1830, the United States was all the rage in Europe. The French government wanted to understand what made the United States tick. So they sent their leading historian, Alexis de Tocqueville, to the United States. He made the trip because the aristocracy was n-e-r-v-o-u-s about this hot new country that had been on the scene for less than 50 years.

The Declaration of Independence had taken the world by storm. The Declaration said:

> WE HOLD THESE TRUTHS TO BE SELF-EVIDENT, THAT ALL MEN ARE CREATED EQUAL, THAT THEY ARE ENDOWED BY THEIR CREATOR WITH CERTAIN UNALIENABLE RIGHTS, THAT AMONG THESE ARE LIFE, LIBERTY AND THE PURSUIT OF HAPPINESS.

This was an unequivocal statement of **equality**, in bold defiance of 80/20.

In his book *Democracy in America,* Tocqueville wrote that this idea of equality, combined with *individualism* (a term he coined to describe the United States) were the two greatest driving forces in America. These forces existed in tension: We are all created equal and have equal rights under the law, yet within our equality we are free to express our individual selves, free to compete, free to become unequal in as many other ways as we wish.

Tocqueville asked the question: "Where did this idea of equality originally come from?" He traced the idea back to St. Paul in the first century who said, "In Christ there is neither male nor female, Jew nor Greek, slave nor free. All are equal."

Nobody before had ever said that. Not that strongly, anyway. Tocqueville observed that equality was an explicitly *spiritual* value and that this idea of equality was rapidly gaining ground everywhere. He predicted that this idea of equality, and some form of democracy, would eventually overtake the world.

There are two things I think are really interesting about this. The first is, prior to the first century, no one would even dare suggest everyone is equal. People were so obviously unequal that to say otherwise was ludicrous.

The second thing is, equality is a *spiritual* value. The founding document of the most successful political system of our time insists that spirituality trumps physical reality. You possess rights because God endowed you with intrinsic value and honor.

People are always trying to mess with this. It doesn't take long before it "evolves":

> WE HOLD THESE TRUTHS TO BE SELF-EVIDENT, THAT ALL MEN ARE ~~CREATED~~ SOMEWHAT EQUAL, THAT THEY ARE ENDOWED BY ~~THEIR CREATOR~~ US WITH CERTAIN ~~UNALIENABLE~~ NEGOTIABLE RIGHTS . . .

80/20 always stands ready to provide a good-sounding excuse for changing the deal. "Come on, folks, let's be realistic. Those orphanages are awfully expensive to maintain. If we just diverted some of those funds to the gifted program . . ."

80/20 can inform you only about physical, material realities. But there are higher realities to consider. A Higher Law. This is why I insist that you must always curb your 80/20 appetites with a healthy dose of humility and spiritual sensitivity. As you grow your business and your career, I encourage you to become more generous with every passing year, to be keenly aware of when to obey 80/20 and when to flagrantly defy it.

Sometimes you need to turn 80/20 upside down. What's that saying? *The meek shall inherit the earth.* What does meek mean? Meek doesn't mean weak. Meekness means *having your power under complete control.*

Meekness is biting your lip when you're sorely tempted to cut someone down to size. Meekness is driving a Suburban to your class reunion when you could've shown up in a $500,000 luxury motor coach.

Dividing Pies vs. Baking New Ones

In Paul Zane Pilzer's eye-opening book *Unlimited Wealth*, he reports the textbook definition of economics: "The study of the distribution of scarce resources." The dictionary is slightly less onerous: "The social science that deals with the production, distribution, and consumption of goods and services."

These definitions are incomplete at best.

Pilzer explains that the essence of economics is *alchemy*: Lead into gold; creating something from nothing. Turning sand into Pentium chips. Turning a grassy field into a farm and crops. Transforming immaterial ideas into software and websites. Converting chaos into order.

Even agriculture is alchemy. DNA, water, and sunlight transform dirt into corn and grass. Corn and grass turn sperm into cows. DNA is instructions for turning minerals into living creatures and food. DNA is information. It's an idea, a plan written in digital code.

Ideas are the basis of all creative acts.

Thus the most important resources for modern alchemists—you and me—are *knowledge, imagination,* and *inspiration.* I had a conversation with Richard Koch where he said it's *human energy* that creates the magic.

You can't change the 80/20 Power Curve, but you can push the whole thing upward. Don't forget that centuries ago, most people in the world went to bed hungry. So many women died in childbirth, populations succumbed to famine and smallpox. Today, people at the poverty line enjoy more comforts than kings and queens of long ago. That's alchemy. This should be all the reason you need to be optimistic about the future, instead of getting seduced by the negativity and panic of the news media.

An interior decorator walks into every room and considers how she'd re-do the furnishings, paint, and decorations. A contractor drives by a dilapidated house, re-arranges everything in his mind and says, "I fixed it!" Everywhere you go, every business you walk in to, you think of ways to improve their traffic, their conversion, their economics.

YOU are a builder, a developer, an improver, an alchemist. You can't walk into a pub or visit a website or buy a product or let the lawn service guy into your house without considering this.

True Marketing Maniacs and Economic Alchemists generate powerful ideas everywhere they go. And *you* are an alchemist.

Create. Invent. Imagine.

Apply 80/20 in every way you can, and create wealth in such a way that the world is a better place because you have lived.

PARETO SUMMARY

▷ Life for the bottom 20 percent is harsh.

▷ 80/20 taken to a ridiculous extreme is mercenary. No one likes living in a Darwinian world.

▷ Equality is a higher, spiritual value.

▷ Charity is an inside job.

▷ The place you earn in the top 5 percent is an opportunity to be generous to the bottom 20 percent.

Finally Achieving Breakthrough

Joshua Boswell is a consultant in Kansas City, Missouri, and a member of Roundtable, my highest-level mastermind group. Joshua relates this story:

"How could this be happening . . . again?"

It was December. Our thermometer, hanging off the eaves outside the kitchen window, had read 21 degrees as I passed it on the way to the car parked on the road behind our little house in Helena, Montana. I thought, "Yeah, but that's before you add in the wind chill factor." I could feel my nose freezing.

The cold outside was nothing compared to the iceberg inside my chest.

Numbly, I opened the car door and climbed in. I didn't bother to start it. I was supposed to head to a meeting, but a phone call a few minutes before was a sledgehammer to my skull. It crushed whatever semblance of clear thinking I had left.

"I thought I was past this. This is like 2001 all over again . . . except worse. What am I going to tell my wife, Margie?"

Five years before, in 1999, I founded a new company with two business partners. We used database connections to make content on the internet both dynamic and highly localized. For its time, it was brilliant.

I was the CEO, marketing guy, web designer, copywriter, negotiator, sales trainer, investor relations department, and accountant. I was the only one of the three partners that didn't have a "real job." So I was doing **everything**.

I convinced an investor to give us some dough. On September 13, 2001, we were slated for our second round of funding. Even though it was tough, and I was doing everything, I was riding on top of the world . . .

At least that is what I was telling the investor and my partners. The truth was, I was holding body and soul together with charisma and force of personality. Most everything I did was half-baked. I didn't have time, energy, or skill to do it all, *all of the time.*

On September 11th, terrorists slammed jets into the Twin Towers, and the world changed. Our would-be investor had offices in New York. He lost much money and several good friends that day. There was no way he was inking a deal with us on the 13th. As the company's accountant, I'd stretched funds and resources so tight that without the flux of funding, we were dead.

Eighteen months later, we folded. I was left holding $12,000 of personal debts and some unhappy business partners. It was one of the hardest experiences possible.

Or so I thought . . .

As I sat in my frigid car trying to push back the blackness, I thought, "2001 was nothing. I'd take that over this any day."

Two years earlier, I'd discovered I had a gift: system acceleration. When I focused on existing systems and businesses, I could instantly see what was wrong and how to twist a few dials and fix it.

By changing two things, nonprofits could more than double their average contribution and nearly triple new-donor acquisition rates. I helped some local politicians and nonprofits execute these changes. It cost them little, and the results were immediate.

One small, statewide organization brought in over 10,000 new donors and almost tripled donations in three months, by adding two sentences and a return envelope to their thank-you letters.

A political candidate raised as much money in three weeks as he had in the previous 14 months (well over a million dollars) by making one small change to his donor pledge fulfillment.

I showed my results to national organizations that I was passionate about. An investor gave me two rounds of funding so that I could build a call center and mail house that could handle national accounts.

Not realizing the failure of my web technology startup mostly came from me trying to do everything, I once again took the company's reigns. I embarked on my journey as CEO, salesman, accountant, copywriter, list broker, mail shop manager, call center designer, and trainer.

First, I focused on closing clients. They lined up like hungry teenagers on pizza night, and in a few months, I had over 20 national accounts. Then I turned my attention to finding simple, inexpensive shifts that would spike their revenues. I could always find a few.

Then, I shifted to managing the company and delivering on the promises I'd made.

That's when hell seemed to unleash her fury. Obviously *I* was the problem. I did not have the ability, resources, or the skills to do everything. I could write the copy for the letters and call scripts, but the labeling, mail shop work, database management, employee training, etc, was killing me.

The call on that cold night was a confirmation of what I already knew: "Joshua, we're going out of business. The last day of our call center will be Monday."

Only this time, I had over 30 employees and an investor who would soon be demanding repayment of his six-figure investment, which I had naively personally guaranteed.

Just at the moment when I felt like I would either go mad or freeze to death, a loud voice shouted in my mind, "Joshua, just start the car and go to your meeting. It will be all right."

I don't know why I obeyed that voice, but I did. It yanked me out of my paralysis, and I attended my meeting. I hoped something magical would happen there, but no solution presented itself that day.

Soon after, I received a letter telling me that if I took a home study course on copywriting and being a marketing consultant, I could make six figures working at home in my PJs.

I was tempted to throw it away, but that familiar voice in my head said I should buy the course. I borrowed money from my father-in-law, because we were financially destitute, and got started.

Margie and I assessed what had gone wrong with all my other business ventures: I'd consumed most of my energy doing things I was naturally ill-equipped to do.

We vowed that this time around, it would be *different*.

Yes, I was a decent writer, but I ALWAYS won when I sold in person. I could almost always find tiny 80/20 levers of persuasion that swung huge response.

For the next year, I focused on finding and closing clients, then locating the small hinges that swung big doors. I didn't hire the employees. I didn't design the websites (I bought a template and filled in the blanks). I didn't run the books.

I just sold, EVERYWHERE. In person, one the phone, LIVE, whatever it took!

Yes, I wrote for my clients, but even then, I would just pretend I was selling face-to-face, record the conversation, and transcribe it.

(Later, when I took Perry's Marketing DNA Test, I scored 8 out of 10 on LIVE and 9 out of 10 on EMPATHY. I should have been spending my time selling live in person all along. If only I'd taken the test 10 years sooner!)

Also, even though I was selling myself as a copywriter, once I had the deal, I quickly moved the conversation into my other uniqueness zone: *accelerating systems.*

I created a three-question system for discovering needs and system weaknesses. I called it the "Easy Conversation" because it facilitated natural, relaxed meetings that produced tens of millions of dollars for my clients and hundreds of thousands of dollars for me.

Just over a year after that freezing night in December, I hung up the phone and leaned back at my desk, grinning like the Chesire Cat. Margie, my amazing wife, walked in just at that moment.

"You look like you just got the deed to all the real estate in Manhattan. What's up?"

"Margie, I called the direct line for Tim Sawyer, global VP of marketing for Corel! He's my new friend. We both love skiing, our children, traveling. He insisted that I work on their next major product launch."

It was a targeted effort to win police-department business back from Adobe. Forensic units use photo-editing software to analyze crimes scene photos. Adobe controlled 90 percent of the market, and Corel wanted a piece of the pie.

My job was to get it for them.

I found a small, obscure feature in PaintShop Pro that PhotoShop did not have: change tracking. Each time any change was made—anything at all—PaintShop Pro recorded and stamped it with time, date, IP address, MAC address, and username if the person was logged in.

This seemed irrelevant until I interviewed forensic officers and heard the term "chain of custody." With the rising use of digital photography, departments across the country were losing cases because they could not prove that the photos had not been tampered with. Judges were throwing out the cases.

We built a package around that one simple phrase. In a few months, we snatched up more than 25 percent of the market, scoring $10 million in new contracts.

Then, Corel brought me back to help them with the global launch of a new product and the global release of two other products. Things were really heating up!

This time, my 80/20 lever was list segmenting. They had been mailing the exact same promotion to millions of customers. I showed them how to segment their file with Recency, Frequency, Money—tailoring the message to specific subgroups. That would slash waste, and spike response and revenues.

We created over 85 list segments and customized each message by no more than one or two paragraphs. The result was a 70 percent open rate and a 59 percent increase in overall sales.

That tiny change cost so little time and not much money but triggered tens of millions of dollars in sales.

I've since applied my two unique capabilities—selling live and accelerating systems—at companies like Toshiba, Corel, Sony, Microsoft, St. Jude's Children's Fund, Catholic Near East Relief Service, Christian Children's Fund, and dozens of others—the big names!

I found other ways to multiply myself. I discovered that when selling from the stage, I could make as much in a 90-minute presentation as I could in three to four months of consulting or writing copy.

At one event, I gave a 60-minute presentation. I closed over 80 percent of the room on a $6,500 product and generated more than half a million in sales. So much better than stuffing envelopes and haggling with employees, don't you think?

That has all been great. My favorite 80/20 story is rescuing a small Christian private school in small-town Utah.

Quin was a brilliant boy with blazing red hair, one of those kids who's always throwing baseballs through windows and dousing GI Joes in kerosene. When he was six, a counselor in public school doped him up with Ritalin to break his spirits and "keep order in the classroom."

His parents pulled him out and placed him in private school. Quin's teachers "got" him. They channeled his energy and helped him express his creative genius. He thrived under their mentorship.

The founder invited me on the board. During our first board meeting, I discovered something was terribly wrong. The global financial crisis had not been kind to private schools. Enrollment dropped sharply.

If something didn't change, the school would close, forcing Quin to go back into public school, where he would return to being a misfit instead of a genius.

They needed a targeted, emotionally charged direct-mail campaign. But the school had no *dinero*. Not even enough to send a few hundred letters.

I got on the phone and personally called the top ten wealthiest families in the school. Each was invited to a special five-course meal catered by a gourmet chef. At the end of dinner, I made a presentation and outlined the school's dire situation. Before the night was over, the school had $15,000, in hand, with a pledge for twice that if needed.

It wasn't needed. We spent only $5,000, and they kept the rest for immediate expenses.

I built the campaign using my fundraising method. Within a week, enrollment doubled. A large waiting list ensured the next few years would be just fine.

As beautiful as that was, little did I know how crucial saving the school would later be to Quin and his family.

Five months later, *en route* to a business meeting, Quin's dad's private plane was struck by lightning and crashed into a lake. All four passengers were killed.

Quin's mom was pregnant with their fifth child at the time. Her world blew apart, threatening to destroy Quin and his siblings as well. In those dark hours, it was the staff and other parents from the private school that rallied around Quin's family. We became her support, love, rock, and strength.

Moms and dads organized and provided meals, rides to school, activities, counseling, tutoring.

I and others reached out to Quin and his brothers and sisters. While we could never take their father's place, we took them under our wing.

Today Quin has grown into a respectful, well-rounded, responsible, enterprising young man. He is what he is today because in a crisis, his schoolmates and their parents rallied around him. *Those people would not have been there for Quin had the school shut its doors.*

I witnessed a miracle that year. It was a miracle that would not or could not have happened if Quin had been just another ADHD kid sentenced to a state-run educational prison with 500 other edu-clones.

The school stayed open for one reason: 80/20. Those knife-edge pivot points tilted everything. They sure transformed Quin's world.

80/20 levers are everywhere. Kids like Quin are all around you! Outstanding products, services and schools, and talented people languish in an acid bath of mediocrity, dying to be discovered.

They don't know how to escape it. **You do.**

I don't know you, but here's what I do know about you: You're one of the few who made it all the way to the end of this book. That alone puts you in elite company; it demonstrates a high level of commitment. Only you can choose to implement the strategies that will put you in the top 1 percent.

Armed with the tools in this book, *you* can make the difference. You can make more money, close more sales, win more clients. With less work, less stress, and greater satisfaction.

Some people get exponentially worse with increasing financial problems. They wither away, broke and destitute. Others grow exponentially wealthier, gaining vigor and vitality as they get older.

The only difference is that the latter group decided to harness the natural power of 80/20 and eliminate the 80 percent of the trivia in their lives.

But YOU have to do it. You have to put it in action. Only you can put on your 80/20 lenses and choose to see the world in a new way. Only you can harness your top 1 percent. Only you can serve the Quins in your life. You can use your brawn, or you can use your brain. Your fate is in your hands. You alone can decide to make more by working less.

Don't sell *harder*. Market **smarter**.

The Story Behind the Story

March 21, 2003, is burned into my memory. Richard Koch's book *The 80/20 Principle* had set my mind on fire just a few weeks before. I had been immediately struck with an insight: "80/20 isn't just a theory about 'Group A' and 'Group B,' it's a calculus formula. It's a ramplike curve. It's infinite, and it's fractal."

That day was a Friday, and I was obsessing about it. What's this formula? How would you set it up? How would you solve it? I was rolling it around in my mind, trying to figure it out. Just two days earlier, something else remarkable happened. I'd hosted a single teleseminar, which generated over $11,000 of sales in one hour, which at the time was an almost miraculous amount of money.

I was thinking, "How could I use my business to help Alan's project in Mozambique?" A relative was building a school there for children. Mozambique was the 18th poorest country in the world—most people there existed on a dollar a day, and those kids had *nothing*. So all day long I was thinking about two things: 80/20 math and Mozambique.

That night my wife encouraged me to go hear some music at our church. The music is playing, and I'm a million miles away—in la-la land. I'm dreaming of 80/20 formulas and thinking about Mozambique, and . . .

Out of the corner of my eye, I see a woman making a beeline for me. I've never seen her before. She marches right up to me, sticks out her hand, and says "Hi, my name is Vivian, and the Lord gave me a word for you."

Huh?? I've heard of stuff like this but never experienced it.

She says, "The Lord told me that you are very, very good at math, and you are working on some kind of formula, some kind of equation. Some kind of . . ." she struggles to find the right word ". . . invention." I look around. *How many people in this room are trying to solve a math problem—right this minute?*

She continues, "And you're going to figure it out. You just keep working at it and keep working at it, cuz you're gonna figure it out!" She turns to walk away. Suddenly she wheels back around. "Oh, and He told me something else. You want to support missions. God is going to bless your business so you can support missions."

OK . . . she got the math part right. Invention is even the right word for it. Not too many people listening to this hippie music gig could possibly be inventing math formulas right now. But how did she know I had a business?

I stared at her, overcome with emotion. I said, "If you only knew."

She flashed me the brightest smile you've ever seen, pointed up in the air and said, "He knows!"

Then she turned and walked away. Just like that.

I'd heard rumors of such things, but suddenly this had happened to me. No honest statistician could chalk that up to coincidence. A "Memo from the Head Office." Unmistakable. I'd been entertaining doubts about God, but I'd have to be in abject denial to shrug this off.

I continued to chip away but kept coming up empty, over and over. I would search the web and couldn't find anything quite like it. I rolled it around in my mind. I'd work at it, put it on the shelf, then come back every now and then and try again. Time passed.

Three years later, I was sitting in a Roundtable meeting, refereeing a dozen wooly entrepreneurs who act as each others' informal board of directors. I was doodling on a scratch pad. Epiphany! Suddenly I saw how to set up the equations. The 80/20 Power Curve was born.

It went through several iterations. For years I used it for myself and with clients to make predictions and solve problems. It evolved into the 8020curve.com tool you've seen in this book.

A few months after that day in March 2003, my business hit the proverbial "hockey stick." 500 percent growth in two years, a magic carpet ride with books selling like crazy and speaking invitations were rolling in.

Much later, I remembered what Vivian had said and wondered: "Did anything *interesting* happen that week?" I combed through some old emails. On the previous Tuesday, Ken McCarthy had sent me a note: "Perry, I need someone to speak at my seminar on Google AdWords. I think that person should be you."

At the time, Ken's System Seminar was Action Central of the online marketing space, a magnet for the best and brightest. The conference accurately forecasted every major trend in internet marketing from email marketing to video to mobile.

I had never seriously considered writing or teaching AdWords until Ken's invitation came. AdWords was new and few people understood it. I wrote the very first version that I sold at that seminar which evolved into *Ultimate Guide to Google AdWords* and offered it at Ken's seminar.

Shortly after that, Google went supernova. Nobody at the time had any idea that this eccentric, idealistic company from Mountain View, California, was about to become the 800-pound gorilla of the internet. My career lurched forward. I never imagined that my new book would eventually become the world's best-selling book on internet advertising.

That one speaking invitation, which came three days before I met Vivian, put me on the map. I was prepared, I had honed my marketing chops, and my business exploded—just like she had predicted.

From that point forward, I understood two things: 1) You take care of the poorest of the poor and He's gonna take care of you, and 2) when you need wisdom . . . ASK.

At the beginning of this book is a dedication: "To the Master Mathematician, and to Vivian." I'm thankful to Vivian for boldly stepping out and talking to a guy who thought she might be crazy. As for the Master Mathematician, He knows how to solve everything. He's also a Master Entrepreneur and CEO.

Do you need help growing your business? Just ask.

The Power Curve and 80/20 for Math Geeks

By Perry Marshall and Brian Woodruff

Have you ever experienced a flash realization as a thousand connections suddenly raced across your brain? The unfamiliar becomes familiar because you recognize that a new thing is just like something else you already knew?

That's what happened to me. When I "discovered" 80/20, I experienced two immediate epiphanies, one right after another:

1. "80/20 is *fractal!*" Zoom in or zoom, out, the shape and pattern are exactly the same.
2. "80/20 is not two groups—"these" and "those." It's a continuous curve and calculus formula. Because it's fractal, the curve looks exactly the same whether we're describing a basketball tournament or the Forbes 400.

It took me a couple of years to decipher the formula. It is now embodied in the Power Curve at 8020curve.com. In this Appendix, I'd like to take it a few steps further and reveal some fascinating truths.

The 80/20 Curve has been everywhere, all around you, all your life. That's why 80/20 is the most important math you can know in business. It's literally the very next thing anyone should learn after addition, subtraction, multiplication, and division. "Power Laws," as mathematicians call them, are actually more useful in daily life than algebra and geometry.

Power Laws are for everyman. But for some reason Power Laws have been relegated to advanced statistics classes and obscured by esoteric language. I was taught next to nothing about Power Laws in college, even though as an electrical engineer I had to take 23 credit hours of advanced mathematics, including a course in probability.

Fractals are fascinating, and they are everywhere. The reason I recognized the truth about 80/20 so clearly was because my wife once checked out a book on fractals for me at the library (*The Beauty of Fractals* by Heinz-Otto Peitgen and Peter Richter, Springer-Verlag, 1986). The zoom-in, zoom-out pattern of 80/20 was deeply familiar. I recommend you read the section on fractals in the supplement at www.perrymarshall. com/8020supplement.

My audio background also contributed to this insight, because my first job after college was designing speakers. In sound, almost everything— including notes on the piano, octaves, and decibels—is logarithmic. Octaves are powers of two; a 10-decibel increase in sound is a 10-times increase in power. I recognized Power Laws because so many of my engineering classes incorporated exponentials ("e^x") in so many math formulas.

In the next few pages I'm going to connect the 80/20 Principle I've espoused in this book to additional concepts in mathematics and also show you some fascinating patterns. Let's start with the patterns.

Armed with the 80/20 Power Curve, You Can Glean Volumes of Insight from Simple, Ordinary Statistics

Let's say you're reading the newspaper and it says, "Southwest Airlines, the world's 167th largest company with revenues of $15.7 billion . . ." Guess what: You already know enough to size up the entire Fortune 500. You even know the total output of the Fortune 500 with a shocking degree of accuracy. All you need is the Power Curve, and it will tell you everything else.

We look up the Fortune 500 list and confirm that Southwest is Number 167. We then plug that number into the app on 8020PowerCurve.com:

1. Click on the tab that says "Report individual member."
2. Enter Number of members = 500 (there are 500 members of the Fortune 500).
   Rank of individual member = 167 (Southwest is Number 167).
   Output of individual member = $15.7 (billion).
3. Then click "Calculate Other Members." Here's what you get:

Figure A–1 estimates the size of all the rest of the Fortune 500 companies. What's reality? In Figure A–2, page 212 here's the same graph with *Fortune* magazine's actual stats plotted alongside:

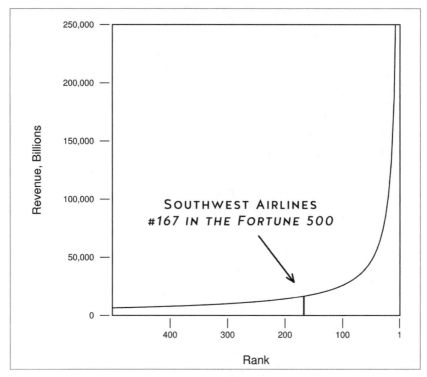

Figure A–1. Predicted revenue of the Fortune 500, based on company Number 167, Southwest Airlines, which is marked on the graph.

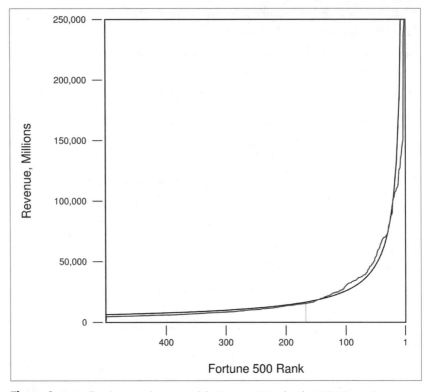

Figure A–2. Predicted vs. actual revenue of the Fortune 500, using the 80/20 Power Curve.

Considering that this was generated from one lone statistic on only one company and we didn't do anything to enhance or massage the data, it's pretty impressive. Most of the time all you need to do is switch from 80/20 to 70/30 or 90/10, and the curve fits pretty well.

For phenomena involving millions of people I find 75/25 seems to be about right much of the time. Given that the tool is completely generic, yet in many situations is accurate to +/-25 percent across hundreds or even millions of members, attests to the universal applicability of the 80/20 Power Curve.

How large is the total output of the Fortune 500? The tool predicts $14.3 trillion. Reality: $11.7 trillion. Theory is less than 25 percent off the mark, and we generated this estimate from ONE number from one newspaper article about one company. Scary.

If you know any two of these things . . .

- Total number of members
- Number of members who responded
- Mean or median output
- Individual rank
- Individual output

. . . you can predict the others because 80/20 is truly a law of nature.

In Figure A–3, here's a graph of the sizes of all cities in the United States, right next to a 70/30 Power Curve:

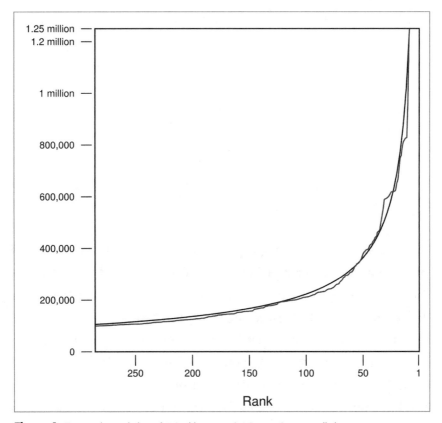

Figure A–3. Actual population of U.S. cities vs. 80/20 Power Curve prediction.

Figure A–4 on page 214 shows the top 100 members of the Forbes 400 Billionaires list. The data is from www.forbes.com/billionaires/list/. When you set the 8020curve.com tool to 60/40, it matches so close it's scary:

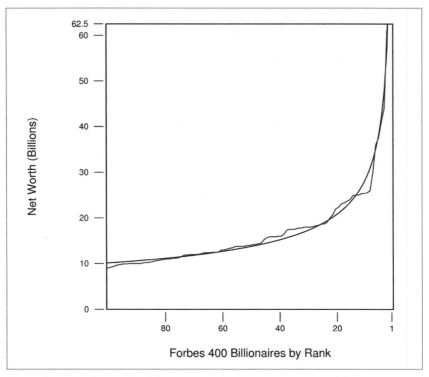

Figure A–4. Actual net worth of the Forbes 400 vs. 80/20 Power Curve prediction.

And in Figure A–5 on page 215 a graph of milk production of 38 counties in the state of Wisconsin, right next to the 80/20 Power Curve. (Data source: www.nass.usda.gov/Statistics_by_State/Wisconsin/ Publications/Annual_Statistical_Bulletin/page40-41.pdf)

Here's a graph of 29 donations to a church within a period of time, ranging from $10 to $12,500, shown in Figure A–6, page 216. This was supplied to us by Jeff Jibben of ParadoxPlants.org.

Whether we count the animals in the top 100 zoos in the world, or the traffic on all the pages on Wikipedia, or the square footage of office buildings in Des Moines, Iowa, the numbers hold and the curves fit. The 80/20 Curve is the most universal pattern in your life that no one ever pointed out until now.

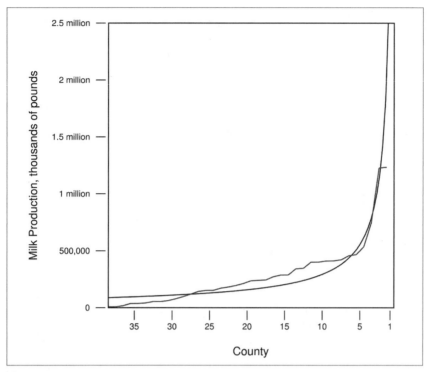

Figure A–5. Actual milk output of 38 Wisconsin counties vs. prediction by the 80/20 Curve.

The Asymptote

The 80/20 curve extends up, up, up, never actually reaching the right side. If you have an infinite number of members, the most productive one will have infinite output. Infinity squared! Fractals are strange and wonderful.

Anomalies

The "King Effect" says that the "kings," the members at the very top, often vary wildly. The top one to three members of a population will often be oddballs. They grab your attention.

The quintessential example of the King Effect is the salaries for the Chicago Bulls during the '97–'98 season. Do you notice that a particular team member stands out from the rest?

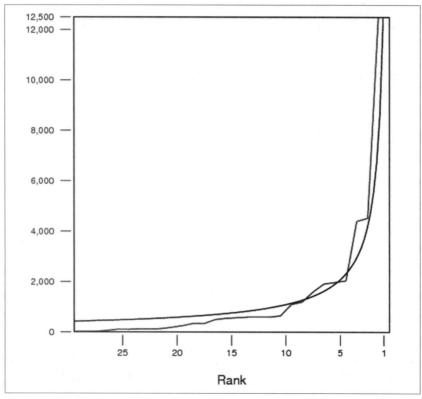

Figure A–6. Donations to a church vs. prediction by the 80/20 Curve.

Michael Jordan $33,140,000
Toni Kukoc $4,560,000
Ron Harper $4,560,000
Dennis Rodman $4,500,000
Luc Longley $3,184,900
Scottie Pippen $2,775,000
Bill Wennington $1,800,000
Scott Burrell $1,430,000
Randy Brown $1,260,000
Dickey Simpkins $1,235,000
Robert Parish $1,150,000
Jason Caffey $850,920
Steve Kerr $750,000
David Vaughn $693,840

Keith Booth $597,600

Jud Buechler $500,000

Joe Kleine $272,250

Rusty LaRue $242,000

(Source: www.examiner.com/article/the-best-chicago-bulls-team-ever)
Why does Michael Jordan make five times more than the next guy on the
list? Because he sells more tennis shoes, more TV commercials, more hats and
T-shirts and packed sports arenas than everyone else put together.

Another illustration of the King Effect is world population. Figure A–7
is from the Wikipedia entry "King Effect":

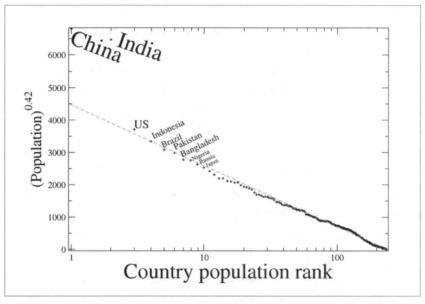

Figure A–7. If you plot world population on a log scale, the countries fall on a straight line. This
illustration is highest to lowest, instead of lowest to highest, as is normal in the rest of this book.

This curve shows both size and rank on a logarithmic scale (powers of
10). Every country is very close to the straight line, but you see that China
and India are both bigger than the Power Laws predict. This is the King
Effect in operation. In any 80/20 or Power Law phenomenon, when you
plot both axes on a log scale, you get a straight line.

This grants you **hugely** powerful insight into almost any situation. I
didn't want to spend time blathering about logarithms in a business book

intended for sales and marketing people, but the fact that you're reading this appendix probably means you're not the average bear.

If you understand logs and powers of 10, you now understand that **everything in business and sales and marketing, and the math of what drives the world, is exponential and logarithmic**. In business you MUST think in powers of 10 in order to see the world accurately, to size up opportunities and make sound judgments.

Yeah, I know, most people aren't math wizards. But I know 20 percent of the people in the world—and probably 30 to 40 percent of the people reading this book—are "numbers people." If you understand both math and business and this doesn't get your blood pumping, I don't know what will.

The kind of math I'm describing here is classified as "Pareto Distributions." Pareto curves are usually presented backward from the way my 80/20 Curve is oriented. In Pareto curves, the value rises as you go from right to left. I think left to right is much more intuitive.

Another way of describing the logarithmic pattern of Power Laws is "Zipf's Law." Zipf's Law says that the actual strength of a member is inversely proportionate to its rank. So if book Number 10,000 on Amazon is selling 20 copies a day, book Number 100,000 is probably selling one-tenth as many—two copies a day. It says that if the 100th most popular word in English is "us," then "southern," the 1,000th most popular word, will be one-tenth as common

This is approximately true. 80/20 is actually a bit more accurate than that. In 80/20, the rule of thumb is:

- Five times the people will spend one-fourth the money.
- One-fifth the people will spend four times the money.
- Ten times the people will spend one-seventh the money.
- One-tenth the people will spend seven times the money.
- One 100th of the people will spend 50 times the money.
- 100 times the people will spend one-fiftieth as much money.

In English, word number 10 is 50 times more popular than word number 1,000. Word frequencies in any language also obey Zipf's Law. The handy rule of thumb is to just assume that it's 100 times more popular. The math becomes super easy, and you're still only off by 50 percent.

So if you have 100 customers who've spent $10,000 each, you can be certain that one of them can spend a million dollars. Or at least half a million. This is almost inevitably true; all you have to do is put the right offer in front of them.

The least accurate end of the 80/20 Curve is usually the bottom. If 100 of your customers have spent $10,000 each, the 80/20 Curve says that a million people will spend $4. That may very well be true. But that could also be ridiculous. If you run a car dealership and you sold 100 cars last month for $10,000 apiece, I can assure you that a million people somewhere did in fact spend four bucks on their transportation. Maybe they took the train. But they didn't spend it with you, and there's no way you could attract or do business with a million people with a four-dollar transaction.

I've seen many markets where 80/20 stops working below a certain price range. Just because you got 100 people into your $5,000 seminar doesn't guarantee that you can get 10,000 people to buy your $50 DVD set. This is especially true of markets where participation requires "total commitment." A person with cancer is nearly as likely to spend $10,000 out of his own pocket on a chemotherapy treatment as he is to buy and read a $10 book.

In some markets, the half-committed just aren't worth selling to. Another reason might be: your 100 seminar participants were drawn from a very high quality referral source, and you don't have direct access to a wider universe of 10,000 people.

80/20 is based on feedback, and the number-one reason the numbers break down on the bottom end of the curve is that at some threshold, the feedback loop is completely broken. Theory says that out of 1,000 people, the bottom guy in the room should make $8,000 per year. But he actually makes nothing because of a disability.

In my experience, 80/20 sometimes breaks down as you go *down* in price. But it almost *always* holds as you go *up* in price.

Life as Number One vs. Number Two vs. Number Three

Even considering King Effect, 80/20 is very accurate. And it's really interesting to see how the numbers shake out. 80/20 says:

If Player number one produces 100, then . . .

Player number two produces 55
Player number three produces 38
Player number four produces 30
Player number five produces 25.

Again, the King Effect says how number one and number two turn out can be wildly erratic, but the numbers above describe the most typical pattern. The number-one player is almost twice as large and influential as the number-two player and four times better than number five. And I can attest to you, based on all my defeats and victories in business, based on my observations from consulting in over 300 industries: Life in the top position is far easier than number five. At position five you're fighting over the scraps with everyone else. When you're number one, the world eats out of your hand.

This also illustrates *the principle of the slight edge.* You win by a narrow margin but the rewards are huge. The difference between number one and number two in the Olympics may be 0.1 second but the rewards could be millions.

PARETO SUMMARY

▷ Five times the people will spend one-fourth the money.
▷ One-fifth the people will spend four times the money.
▷ Almost everything that matters in business is exponential.
▷ The very bottom of the 80/20 curve sometimes over-estimates output.
▷ The number-one player is sometimes wildly more powerful than the others. This is called the King Effect.

■ ■ ■

The formulas and algorithms behind the 80/20 Power Curve were developed by me and Brian Woodruff. They are proprietary and available under license. To make an inquiry, submit a support ticket at www.perrymarshall.com, and someone on my team will make an appointment to discuss it with you.

Brian Woodruff is a wizard at analyzing customers and data. If you want Brian to find 80/20s in your customer or website traffic data, contact my office.

About the Author

Entrepreneur magazine says, "Perry Marshall is the number-one author and world's most-quoted consultant on Google Advertising. He has helped over 100,000 advertisers save literally billions of dollars in AdWords stupidity tax."

He's consulted in over 300 industries, from computer hardware and software to high-end consulting, from health and fitness to corporate finance. He's one of the world's most expensive and sought-after marketing consultants. Prior to his consulting career, he helped grow a tech company from $200,000 to $4 million in sales in four years. The firm was sold to a public company in 2001 for $18 million.

His works include the world's most popular book on Google advertising, the *Ultimate Guide to Google AdWords*, and the *Ultimate Guide to Facebook Advertising*. He's been featured at conferences in the United States, Canada, United Kingdom, Israel, Australia, and China.

Acknowledgments

Special thanks to:

Laura Marshall, Vivian Gaulding, Brian Woodruff, Boyan Mihaylovy, Richard Koch, Ken McCarthy, John Paul Mendocha, Dan Kennedy, Jay Abraham, Bill and Steve Harrison, Bill Glazer, Bryan Todd, Gary Bencivenga, Brian Kurtz, John Carlton, Stan Dahl, Glenn Livingston, Alex Mandossian, Scott Martineau, Clate Mask, Jack Born, Matt Gillogly, Bob Boldt, Danielle Flanagan, Jeremy Flanagan, Lorena Ybarra, Phil Alexander, Larry Benet, Gypsy Rogers, Geoff Vautier, Dave Dee, Andy Mason, Ari Galper, Rich Schefren, David Bullock, Dr. James Kowalick, Sunny Hills, Jillian McTeague, Karen Billipp, Jeff Herman, Smriti Maity, the folks at Buzz Cafe, Joe Polish, Darcy Juarez, Bob Regnerus, Tim Ferriss, Ben Morris, Tom Meloche, Drew Bischof, David Frey, Jonathan Mizel, Paul Lemberg, Ivan and Isabel Allum, Steve and Dawna DeSilva, Alan Pieratt, John and Jay Fancher, Howard Jacobson, Don Crowther, Shelley Ellis, Brad Geddes, Andrew Goodman, Charley Martin, Dan Sullivan, Ian Carroll, Nate and Laura Jennison, Robert and Virginia Knoll, Michael Cage, Wally Doctor, Fred Roediger, Mike Justice, John Fox, Dream Chicago, the crew at GCC, Robin and Ted Eschliman, Ron and Eileen Pieratt, and Mom and Dad.

Index